AN EARTHFUL

AN EARTHFUL *of* GLORY

Biblical prayers, liturgies and meditations

J. PHILIP NEWELL

First published 1996
SPCK
Holy Trinity Church
Marylebone Road
London NW1 4DU

British Library Cataloguing in Publication Data

A catalogue record for this book is available from the British Library.

ISBN 0-281-04833-9

Scripture quotations are taken from *The New Revised Standard Version of the Bible*
© 1989, sometimes in adapted form.

These services and prayers were compiled by Philip Newell, a Minister of the Church
of Scotland. They are published for use in churches of any denomination in circum-
stances in which the minister has discretion to decide the order of service.

They are not official or authorized liturgies of the Church of England, the Church
of Scotland or any other Christian body.

Typeset by Pioneer Associates, Perthshire
Printed in Great Britain by Arrowsmiths Bristol

To the memory of
George Fielden MacLeod (1895–1991),
The Very Revd Lord MacLeod of Fuinary,
who taught me that matter matters
because at the heart of the material is the
spiritual.

CONTENTS

Contents

PREFACE

I have always felt that the context in which something is written is a key ingredient in the final product. During my time as Warden of Iona Abbey, I wrote *Each Day and Each Night*, a book of prayers that drew heavily on the old Gaelic songs and prayers of the people of the Western Isles. When I moved to St Giles' Cathedral in Edinburgh, I was keen to write again in a way that would reflect something of the history and context of the place in which I was praying, and the particular occasion for beginning to do this was the introduction of a daily communion service at the Cathedral. The return to such a Catholic practice in a building that is both medieval Catholic in its ambience and Protestant in its modern history led me to try to combine the themes of centrality of Scripture and catholicity of worship. These prayers and liturgies are very much a product of this attempt.

And so my thanks are especially due to the people of St Giles', and particularly to Gilleasbuig Macmillan, who in his generous way gave me space and encouragement to write, and whose commitment to worship and utterance of prayer will always be an inspiration to me.

Three other men whom I would like to thank, who are often present to me in my memories of learning and past experience of worship, are Bill Cant, Paul McCarroll and my father, William Newell.

Most of all my thanks are to Alison, who, in the midst of great creativity for us as a family over the last nine months, has also managed to be my most helpful critic and encourager. Without her presence and guidance I could not have written this book.

J. Philip Newell
St Giles' Cathedral

INTRODUCTION

That the earth is full of God's glory, as well as being streaked through with darkness and wrong, is the theme central to this book of prayers, liturgies and meditations. It is a belief reflected also throughout the holy writings of our Christian tradition. Over the last number of years I have been reading and meditating on the Scriptures with an eye to this theme and with the intention of translating key phrases and images from Scripture into use for prayer today, in part as a way of renewing our perspective of the glory of heaven that is interwoven in earth.

Almost without knowing it at first, the method that I was using was that of *lectio divina*, practised as early as the sixth century by St Benedict and by many others over the centuries, in which Scripture is read and particular words pondered as a way of entering contemplation and leading into prayer.

I have become aware of what an immense richness of resource for prayer there is in the common Christian heritage of the Scriptures. Also I have realized afresh how much they are already being used in prayer and worship across the entire spectrum of the Church, whether it is through *lectio divina* and more classical forms of contemplating the Scriptures, the singing of metrical psalms in the Scottish tradition, the chanting of Scripture phrases and the reciting of canticles in High Church liturgies, or whether, as in the more evangelical traditions, it is a committing of Scripture to memory and allowing verses to sink into the inner heart before being used in expressions of personal prayer. I believe that this great treasury can be delved into again and again and imaginatively used in prayer to further awaken within us an awareness of the presence of God in the whole of life. The Scripture translation here used, although sometimes in adapted form, is the *New Revised Standard Version*.

Images from dreams sometimes speak much more powerfully than conscious thought and reasoning. The imagery from three dreams that I have had during the writing of this book graphically reflected for me some of my most strongly held convictions about the relationship between prayer and life. The first image is of a cathedral in which the high walls stretched up into the heavens, with no roof. Below the pulpit was an artificial ceiling under which the people sat. This image speaks of the way in which our prayer and worship are often cut off from the rest of creation and from the world, contained within an artificial separation between the temple of prayer on the one hand and the whole temple of creation on the other. In entering a holy place we do not step aside from life but rather step more deeply into a conscious awareness of the One who is the Life of the world and the Holiness of all life. And so in our words and symbols of offering, in our confessions and seeking of mercy, in our giving voice to thanks and looking for help and new beginnings, in our words and actions of blessing and consecrating, we are to be open in spirit with the whole of creation and even with the whole universe. Our offering is not simply an offering of ourselves for blessing again, but of the entire world. Our song of thanksgiving is not dependent merely upon what we can sing, but rather joins the ongoing song of praise that is happening continuously in the earth and sea and sky around us, in the light of the rising sun in the morning and in the sound of the waves of the sea. Our confession concentrates not in a limited way on the failings of our own lives but is a *kyrie* for the sins of the whole world, just as our yearnings for well-being and peace are not solely for ourselves and our loved ones but for families and people everywhere who look to be delivered from suffering and wrong.

In the second dream, we in the Church had ceased to use our full vision, so much so that we had become one-eyed and our second eye was overgrown by skin and a grotesque covering of hair. This image speaks of a way of seeing that we are in danger of losing entirely if we do not again reclaim it and use it. In our praying, and thus in our living, there is an inner seeing to be recovered that enables us to know the immediacy and the interwovenness of the spiritual within the matter of our lives and our world. Again and again in the Scriptures the world is seen as pervaded by spirit; in and among the people of earth are the messengers of heaven, as well as the principalities of darkness. Creation and humanity are viewed as having been made in the image of God, essentially good and blessed, but are now like occupied territory, under the bondage of evil and yearning for liberation. The twentieth century on the other hand is often fearful of the invisible and of looking into both its heights and its depths. As George MacLeod said, the modern Church has tried to place a seal on the doors of hell, only to hear the doors of heaven clang to. In order to be freed from the imprisonment of a hellish secularism, we need to recover a consciousness of the holy angels of God all around us and undergirding life.

The third dream image is of an altar cloth being pulled in opposite directions. Holding one corner were singers who chanted the most beautiful plainsong. And I dreamt that at the opposite corner, pulling the cloth in the other direction, were members of Amnesty International. The tension on the cloth was so great that the elements could not be placed on the altar, and the Eucharist could not begin. This image speaks of the need to find a balance in prayer between the things of inner silence and renewal and beauty of liturgy, on the one hand, with the imperatives of outward movement and concern and action for suffering on the other. Not only should the direction of prayer and worship be towards a going out, as the *ite missa est* of the mass suggests, exiting in order to give and receive in the world the blessings of Christ that we have celebrated in the mystery of the liturgy, but even within prayer itself there must be a movement from and towards the world. The goodness of the bread and the wine, which earth has given and human hands have made, are part of the gift of life that we have received and then offer again in return to God, just as the sufferings of the world and our own pains are mingled with the wine poured out in the sacrament. And perhaps the most essential element of Christian prayer is a participating in Christ's priesthood for the whole of creation and for all people, making intercession for the life of the world.

The prayers of this book are offered in the hope that, in both our praying and our living, the glory of heaven that is in earth may be seen anew and further set free.

Part One

MORNING AND
EVENING PRAYER

INTRODUCTION

These seven sets of services are written in the tradition of the divine office, prayer at morning and at evening. It was St Benedict who said that the reciting of the office was 'the work of God'. It gives shape and focus to the day, marking its beginning and ending. It can be said individually or collectively, and can be prayed by a lay person alone or led by a priest in church. Its central purpose has always been to pray in the context of reciting the psalms and of reading the Scriptures and reflecting upon them. An essential supplement to a daily office therefore is a lectionary of readings, to act as a guide through the whole of the Scriptures over a period of time. Various lectionaries are available in the major Christian traditions of the West, and increasingly there is movement towards a common use of texts among the churches. The one here recommended is that for Morning and Evening Prayer (Sundays and Weekdays) in *The Alternative Service Book 1980*. Also a very accessible selection of daily lections can be found in *The Lectionary* published annually by SPCK.

There are a number of important tensions to be held on to in a daily office. One which has already been touched upon is that between individual prayer and collective prayer. Both are absolutely essential; they are complementary and interwoven. Since the beginnings of Christian spirituality the practice has been to make use of collective forms of prayer, such as the 'Our Father', even when praying alone. It is part of recognizing that in prayer we join our individual voices to the common and ongoing voice of the Church's prayer, both in heaven and on earth.

Related to this tension is the need also to find a balance between set prayer and free prayer. Whether we pray alone or together it is important to be able to blend general utterances of prayer with very specific expressions which will arise from the world situation and from our lives and relationships. In each service there is provision for free prayer, either to be spoken by the leader, or representatives of the people, or silently offered from the heart. In the prayers of intercession we are able to bring to the service our very specific hopes and fears and concerns. This in turn relates to the balance between praying for others and praying for ourselves, and being aware that the purpose of a daily office is to join Christ in praying for the life of the world, and in that context to pray also for ourselves.

Another area of balance to be sought concerns which voices are to be heard, and when. There is an attempt, for instance, to listen to the voice of both the Old Testament and the New. Also, the voice of traditional prayer, for example in the *kyrie* and *trisagion*, is counterpoised by the voice of newly created prayers, which even in themselves blend both ancient and modern imagery and language. A balance is also desirable in the saying of the canticles, whether they are said responsively between the leader and the people, or antiphonally between different parts of the congregation.

And finally in relation to the tension of voices, we need to seek a balance between sound and silence, whether the sound of word or of music. The tendency is to want to hurry on to the next bit of sound, rather than pausing for silence after the word is read or preached, or after prayers and hymns are spoken and sung. If allowed, the silence will often be the most important part of a service. In being still we may find that we are renewed in the inner heart as we become more and more aware of the One who makes all things new. It is probably better to see words and music as punctuating the silence that is at the core of the service, rather than to see silence as in any sense an appendage to parts of the service.

Each of these morning and evening offices follows a simple fourfold shape. In the first section the blend of Scripture sentence and opening prayer and plea for mercy allows us to move into a more conscious awareness of God, and of the desire, both for ourselves and for the world, to be made whole again.

This is followed immediately by the word section and the

reciting of psalms and canticles and the reading of the Scriptures. Although words and imagery from the Bible are used throughout the office, it is particularly in this section that we listen for the forgiveness and promises and the guidance and revelation of Christ. And whether or not the readings are followed by a sermon, it is important to find ways of being both alert and receptive through reflection and stillness so that the spoken word can settle within us and find its place of deepest acceptance.

Whereas the liturgy of the word is primarily receptive, the thanksgiving and intercessions of the next section turn our gaze outwards. This part of the office, through both structured and free prayer, and spoken as well as silent, combines prayers of giving thanks for the gift of life with prayers that intercede for the brokenness of life. And all our prayers are consummated in joining together to say the 'Our Father'.

The final section, through the reciting of a canticle and a closing prayer and blessing, moves us out and back into the activity of our lives and world, renewed.

The services together form a weekly pattern of morning and evening prayer for each day. This, of course, is not to restrict a particular service to only one point in the week. Each has its own characteristics, which may make it especially suited for use at certain points in the liturgical year or for particular occasions and situations. In Advent, for instance, when readings from the prophet Isaiah are so much in use, there may be a desire to draw more frequently on the morning and evening offices based on Isaiah. And, similarly, sections of particular services can be borrowed to include in other liturgies. Some of the prayers from the Song of Songs services are suited to inclusion in a wedding or in a liturgy in which expression of love and commitment is central.

The services together reflect a variety of themes. The offices based on the prophecies of Isaiah, Jeremiah and Hosea all pick up, in their distinct ways, on themes of justice and prophetic vision, of new beginnings and faithfulness. Similarly, the services inspired by the Wisdom literature, Ecclesiasticus and the Book of Wisdom, reflect an emphasis on the goodness of creation, of God's image within us, and the gift of wisdom and understanding. The Book of Job prayers explore the themes of suffering and of hope in the midst of loss, and the services of the final day, based on the Song of Songs, develop themes of love and passion. While these distinct themes can be found in the different offices, each one is also general enough to be regularly used in a weekly cycle, which together provides a variety of ways of seeing and praying.

DAY ONE
The Prophet Isaiah
Morning Prayer

The earth will be full of the knowledge of the Lord as the
waters cover the sea. *Isaiah 11.9*

Let us pray:

Holy, holy, holy,
Lord God of hosts,
the whole earth is full of your glory
and we bless you,
for you are the Holy and Eternal One
inhabiting the centre of life.
From you the earth comes forth
and all that moves upon it;
from your mystery the heavens unfold
and the lights of the skies shine;
from your vitality flow the depths of the seas,
the waters and creatures of the deep.
You are the first and the last, O God,
the beginning and the end.
By you we have been made,
from your substance we have been formed,
and to you we sing our praise.
Holy, holy, holy!
Let the sea roar and all that fills it,
let the morning dance and all that it awakens,
for we celebrate your glory as here among us
in the great temple of creation.

Morning and Evening Prayer

Lord have mercy upon us.
Christ have mercy upon us.
Lord have mercy upon us.

A HYMN *may be sung*

PSALM

THE FIRST READING (*from the Old Testament*)

SILENCE *may be kept*

CANTICLE
A SONG OF COMFORT

Sing for joy, O heavens, and exult, O earth;
break forth, O mountains, into singing!
For the Lord has comforted his people,
and will have compassion on his suffering ones.
But Zion said, 'The Lord has forsaken me,
my Lord has forgotten me.'
Can a woman forget her nursing child,
or show no compassion for the child of her womb?
Even these may forget,
yet I will not forget you, says the Lord.
Isaiah 49

THE SECOND READING (*from the New Testament*)

SILENCE *may be kept*

A SERMON *may be preached*

PRAYERS OF THANKSGIVING AND INTERCESSION
O Holy One,
above and beyond,
whose ways and thoughts are great

like the heights of the heavens above the earth,
we give thanks that you are also God with us,
that you surround and undergird all life,
and that you are closer to us than our very breath.
For the things of your Spirit
hidden in the depths of the human soul,
and for the wellsprings of salvation
deep in life's landscape
from which in every place and every time
we may draw inner strength,
we offer thanks.
And yet we know also in our lives,
as in all people's lives,
the times and places
when it seems there is no salvation
and the world appears forsaken by your Spirit,
where the earth and its elements lie polluted
and gladness seems banished all around,
where cities are battered into ruins
and nations are torn apart.
For ourselves,
for our loved ones,
and for all people in such places and times,
we pray, O God,
in the sure conviction
that you do not will one of these
to be hurt or destroyed in all your creation.
[*Here free prayer may be offered.*]

THE LORD'S PRAYER
Lord, teach us to pray together:

**Our Father in heaven,
hallowed be your name,
your kingdom come,
your will be done,
on earth as in heaven.**

Give us today our daily bread.
Forgive us our sins
as we forgive those who sin against us.
Lead us not into temptation
but deliver us from evil.
For the kingdom, the power,
and the glory are yours
now and for ever. Amen.

A HYMN may be sung

CANTICLE
A SONG OF SALVATION

Strengthen the weak hands,
and make firm the feeble knees.
Say to those who are of a fearful heart,
Be strong, do not fear!
Here is your God.
He will come with vengeance and save you.
Then the eyes of the blind shall be opened,
and the ears of the deaf unstopped.
Then the lame shall leap like a deer,
and the tongue of the speechless sing for joy.
For waters shall break forth in the wilderness,
and streams in the desert.
Isaiah 35

CLOSING PRAYER
Guide us, O God,
on the unknown paths ahead,
and awaken us to the ever-new thing
that you are bringing forth
in the world and in our lives.
Bless us with understanding
that we may judge,
not merely by what our eyes see

nor by what our ears hear,
but with the wisdom
that decides justly and generously for all.
Grant us the courage and truthfulness
never to call evil good nor good evil,
and a clarity of vision
to see your light shining
even in places of deep darkness.
And glimpsing something of the glory
that will in the end be fully known,
we shall proclaim with confidence, O God,
good news instead of fear,
gladness rather than sighing,
and comfort to those who mourn.

BENEDICTION

The Prophet Isaiah
Evening Prayer

OPENING SENTENCE AND PRAYER
'The mountains may depart and the hills be removed, but my
steadfast love shall not depart from you,' says the Lord.
Isaiah 54.10

Let us pray:

It is in returning to you, O God,
and entering your stillness
that we are renewed,
for in the sure quiet of your peace
is our strength.
Rooted and secured in you

we can hope to bear love's fruits in our lives,
learning to do good and turning from evil.
Our trust is in you,
for like a mother who forgets
the failings of her children,
so you have chosen to forgive.
Outwardly we see many things
but often do not understand,
and our ears are open
but we do not fully hear.
Make us whole again, O God,
that we may see your light all around us
and hear intimations of glory,
which before we had not noticed.
Restored to wholeness by you, O God,
we will sing a new song.

Holy God,
holy and mighty,
holy and immortal,
have mercy upon us.

A HYMN may be sung

PSALM

THE FIRST READING (*from the Old Testament*)

SILENCE may be kept

CANTICLE
A SONG OF NEW STRENGTH

The Lord is the everlasting God,
the Creator of the ends of the earth.
He does not faint or grow weary:
his understanding is unsearchable.

He gives power to the faint
and strengthens the powerless.
**Even youths will faint and be weary,
and the young will fall exhausted.**
But those who wait for the Lord
shall renew their strength, they
shall mount up with wings like eagles.
**They shall run and not be weary,
they shall walk and not faint.**
Isaiah 40

THE SECOND READING (*from the New Testament*)

SILENCE *may be kept*

A SERMON *may be preached*

PRAYERS OF THANKSGIVING AND INTERCESSION

O God, our strength and our salvation,
who hears our prayers
and sees our tears,
who knows our ways
and heals us,
we give thanks for the faithfulness of your love
which has comforted us in sorrow
and assured us in moments of fear.
We pray now for all who are in trouble,
and who know their need:
for those upon whom past mistakes weigh heavily
and who yearn for the freedom of forgiveness
and new beginnings;
for those who are in so much pain
that they have ceased to delight in life;
for those who have lost in an instant
friends or family or home
and are frightened and shocked

in the midst of loss.
Comfort them in their fear
and grant them strength in their weakness.
We pray for those
who are despised and rejected by their own communities,
for the people held of no account
whose sufferings go unattended,
for those who are diseased and wounded
in body or mind or soul,
and for those who suffer oppression of any kind
and bear in their lives the afflictions of injustice.
In prayer we stand with these ones,
asking that their wounds may be healed,
and that we may be part of the binding up of injury
in the world and in one another.
[*Here free prayer may be offered.*]

THE LORD'S PRAYER
Lord, teach us to pray together:

Our Father . . .

A HYMN *may be sung*

CANTICLE
A SONG OF LOVE

Do not fear, for I have redeemed you;
I have called you by name,
you are mine, says the Lord.
When you pass through the waters, I will be with you;
and through the rivers, they shall not overwhelm you.
When you walk through fire you shall not be burned,
and the flame shall not consume you.
For I am the Lord your God,
the Holy One of Israel, your Saviour.

You are precious in my sight, and I love you.
Do not be afraid for I am with you.
Isaiah 43

CLOSING PRAYER
We believe, O God,
that in our going out and coming in,
that in our living and dying,
you are the One who does not forsake us.
We believe that you delight in being among us,
in the dwelling places of men and women everywhere,
in cities and villages
and simple habitations throughout the world.
Inspire and strengthen us
to maintain what is just
and to change what is not right,
to break chains of inhumanity in the world
and be signs of your liberating presence.
It is for your freedom and healing
that we watch and pray, O God,
when the shrouds of darkness
bound round the world
are destroyed
and when tears of sorrow
are wiped away.
Out of life's labour and pain
we look for the rest and the gladness
that you have promised, O God.

BENEDICTION

DAY TWO
The Book of Wisdom
Morning Prayer

I prayed, and understanding was given me; I called on God,
and the spirit of wisdom came to me. *Wisdom* 7.7

Let us pray:

O God, whose spirit fills the world
and holds all things together,
we come as children of the earth
yet created for incorruption,
as born from our mother's wombs
yet made in the image of eternity.
And so we gather
at the start of the day
looking for the light that is brighter than the sun
and the peace that is deeper than night's stillness.
We seek the spirit that never dies,
and which day by day renews the life of the earth.
We seek your gift of wisdom, O God,
which no darkness or power of confusion can overcome,
and pray that in seeking wisdom
we may find it,
and in finding it
find friendship with you.

Lord have mercy upon us.
Christ have mercy upon us.
Lord have mercy upon us.

A HYMN may be sung

PSALM

THE FIRST READING (*from the Old Testament*)

SILENCE *may be kept*

CANTICLE
A SONG OF WISDOM'S GLORY

Wisdom is a breath of the power of God,
a reflection of eternal light,
and an image of his goodness.
In every generation she passes into holy souls
and makes them friends of God, and prophets.
For God loves nothing so much as the person who lives
with wisdom.
She is more beautiful than the sun,
and excels every constellation of the stars.
Compared with the light she is found to be superior,
for the day is succeeded by the night,
but against wisdom evil does not prevail.
Wisdom 7

THE SECOND READING (*from the New Testament*)

SILENCE *may be kept*

A SERMON *may be preached*

PRAYERS OF THANKSGIVING AND INTERCESSION
Blessed are you, O God,
who has called into being all that exists,
and whose creation is good and wholesome.
We give thanks for the great vitality
that stretches from one end of the world to the other,
and from the depths of the seas
to the heights of the heavens,

for the rising of the morning sun
and its unfailing power of light,
for the life-giving rains
that moisten the earth and swell the rivers,
and for all that grows emerging from the ground.
Blessed are you, O God,
for your living spirit breathed into humanity,
for our souls active and inspired by your soul.
That yours is the power over life and over death,
the creativity that brings forth fruit from the soil,
the might that sets free imprisoned spirits,
these things lead us to be bringing our prayers to you:
for all who suffer bondage of any kind,
whether in outward captivity,
bound by physical chains of cruelty and oppression,
or in prisons not made with human hands
where wrongs done are heavier than darkness
and kindness and tenderness seem banished.
From evils that seize us in relationships,
and from haunted inner chambers of our lives
where unexpected fears and temptations
suddenly overwhelm us,
release us we pray.
For ourselves and all people, O God,
hear our prayers for freedom.
[*Here free prayer may be offered.*]

THE LORD'S PRAYER
Lord, teach us to pray together:

Our Father . . .

A HYMN *may be sung*

CANTICLE
A SONG OF BLESSING

Blessed are you, O Lord, God of our ancestors,
to be praised and highly exalted for ever.
Blessed are you in the temple of your glory.
Blessed are you seated among the cherubim,
to be praised and highly exalted for ever.
Blessed are you who look into the depths.
Blessed are you on the throne of your kingdom,
to be praised and highly exalted for ever.
Daniel 3 (Apocrypha)

CLOSING PRAYER
Guide us, O God, on the unknown journey ahead.
Whether it is through blessing or danger,
save us from a deep forgetfulness
that does not remember your guidance in the past
and of many before us.
Like those who passed through the waves of the sea
and through wasteland and wilderness,
guide us too to places of promise
and grant us eyes to see the flame of life
that we are to follow.
May glimmerings of the imperishable light
that glisten within and around us
strengthen our hope in the long-awaited day
when the goodness of creation and your angels of light
will overcome evil
like a mighty tempest winnowing away all wrong.
Then, O God,
the life that is rooted in you
will stand secure.

BENEDICTION

The Book of Wisdom
Evening Prayer

OPENING SENTENCE AND PRAYER
God created us for incorruption, and made us in the image of
his own eternity. *Wisdom 2.23*

Let us pray:

O God who loves everything that lives,
and whose immortal spirit is in all created life,
free us from thoughts that would separate us from you,
from words that harm the soul
and from errors that invite darkness into the world.
From inner confusions over what is good
grant us a clarity of vision,
that we may see your creative wisdom
pervading all things
and each day making life new.
In the stillness of evening,
let us glimpse within us and among us
the light that is an emanation of your glory
that we may be renewed once again, O God,
in the image of your goodness.

**Holy God,
holy and mighty,
holy and immortal,
have mercy upon us.**

A HYMN *may be sung*

PSALM

THE FIRST READING (*from the Old Testament*)

SILENCE may be kept

CANTICLE
A SONG OF THE GIFT OF WISDOM

Wisdom reaches mightily from one end of the earth to
the other,
and she orders all things well.
The mysteries of God have been revealed to her,
and she is an associate in all his works.
If riches are a desirable possession in life,
what is richer than wisdom, the active cause of all things?
And if understanding is effective,
who more than she is fashioner of what exists?
But I perceived that I would not possess wisdom unless God
gave her to me –
and it was a mark of insight to know whose gift she is.
And so I appealed to the Lord,
and implored him with my whole heart.
Wisdom 8

THE SECOND READING *(from the New Testament)*

SILENCE may be kept

A SERMON may be preached

PRAYERS OF THANKSGIVING AND INTERCESSION
We give thanks, O God,
for all that is good
within us,
between us,
and around us,
for the beauty of the sky's constellations,
for patterns of kindness and creativity among people,
for generosities that shine in human lives,
all these things conceived by your wisdom

and from the beginning brought forth in love.
We give thanks that life has flowed from you
and to you returns,
that we are born not of mere chance
to pass like traces of a cloud,
but to share in the eternity of your life,
and that the world is ruled
not by earth's elements and heaven's stars,
but by the wisdom and greatness that created them.
Protect us and all people, O God,
from destructive forces within and without,
from powers that see no meaning
beyond possessing and enjoying.
And grant us eyes to discern
the great spirits of our time
in whom love and wisdom are found,
so that as we seek new beginnings
for ourselves and for our world
we may be guided by their understanding
and by their hope.
[*Here free prayer may be offered.*]

THE LORD'S PRAYER
Lord, teach us to pray together:

Our Father . . .

A HYMN *may be sung*

CANTICLE
THE SONG OF SIMEON

Master, let your servant now depart in peace,
according to your word;
for my eyes have seen your salvation,
which you have prepared in the presence of all peoples,

a light for revelation to the Gentiles
and for glory to your people Israel.
Luke 2

CLOSING PRAYER
Send forth wisdom, O God,
from the heart of your glory,
that she may guide us
in our labours and in our loving.
Let us more and more learn your purposes
and with wisdom understand the world around us,
and as we grow in a knowledge of the human heart
and in our perceptions of what has been and what is,
may we discern also the signs of what is yet to be,
for in the gift of your wisdom, O God,
is the salvation of the world.

BENEDICTION

DAY THREE
The Book of Job
Morning Prayer

OPENING SENTENCE AND PRAYER
In God's hand is the soul of every living thing and the breath of every human being. *Job 12.10*

Let us pray:

O God, who in the beginning created the earth,
and the morning stars sang together
and heavenly beings shouted for joy;
and from whose womb the waters of life came forth,
and grasses grew from the ground
and birds soared in the heights;
and who gave birth to the lights of the skies
and to the movement of the moon in its splendour,
we praise you,
we bless you,
we worship you.
Without your presence
all that has flesh would perish,
all that has breath would return to dust,
and even earth's mountains would crumble,
for it is your life that gives life to all;
it is your spirit that holds all things together,
and so it is to you that we look, O God,
as the source of all our hope.

Lord have mercy upon us.
Christ have mercy upon us.
Lord have mercy upon us.

PSALM

THE FIRST READING *(from the Old Testament)*

SILENCE may be kept

CANTICLE
A SONG OF WISDOM AND UNDERSTANDING

Where shall wisdom be found?
And where is the place of understanding?
God looks to the ends of the earth,
and sees everything under the heavens.
When he gave to the wind its weight,
and apportioned out the waters by measure;
when he made a decree for the rain,
and a way for the thunderbolt;
then he saw wisdom and declared it;
he established it, and searched it out.
And he said to humankind,
'Truly, the fear of the Lord, that is wisdom;
and to depart from evil is understanding.'
Job 28

THE SECOND READING *(from the New Testament)*

SILENCE may be kept

A SERMON *may be preached*

PRAYERS OF THANKSGIVING AND INTERCESSION
We give thanks, O God,
for the gift of life:
for the life that has flowed down to us
from those who have gone before;

for the life that springs up from the earth around us;
and for the life of thought and feeling and imagination
that wells up from within.
As we offer thanks for these signs of life
that have so enfolded us
in the gift of the morning sun,
in the friendship and affection of others,
and in the creativity that emerges from within our souls,
we pray for those who are denied a fullness of life:
for those who are afraid
because of emptinesses within
or uncertainties around them;
for those who are bitter
because of wrongs suffered in the past
or because of a refusal to forgive themselves;
and for those whose hopes have been uprooted
and who have come to loathe life
because of the sufferings they have experienced or seen.
We commend these ones in prayer, O God,
as we pray also for those whom we constantly think of,
for our loved ones and friends.
And what we ask for these ones
we pray also for ourselves,
that more and more we may know your life within us
and within all people,
and be bearers of hope for one another.
[*Here free prayer may be offered.*]

THE LORD'S PRAYER
Lord, teach us to pray together:

Our Father . . .

A HYMN *may be sung*

CANTICLE
A SONG OF RECONCILIATION

Let us give thanks to the Father,
who has enabled us to share in the inheritance of the saints
of light.
He has rescued us from the power of darkness
and transferred us into the kingdom of his beloved Son;
who is the image of the invisible God,
the first-born of all creation.
In him all things in heaven and on earth were created,
things visible and invisible.
And through him all things have been reconciled to God,
by making peace through the blood of his cross.
Colossians 1

CLOSING PRAYER
In both life and death, O God,
you are our health and our salvation.
In all things
strengthen us and enable us
to choose what is right.
May we not be silent
when it is right to speak,
nor speak
when it is wise to be silent.
May we not be content to eat
while those around us have nothing,
nor be satisfied with our safety
while others have no shelter.
And grant us the faith to place our trust
not in the outward securities
of prosperity and possessions,
but in the inner certainty of your love, O God,
deep and true.

BENEDICTION

31

The Book of Job
Evening Prayer

OPENING SENTENCE AND PRAYER
Naked we came from the womb, and naked shall we return
there; the Lord gives, and the Lord takes away; blessed be the
name of the Lord. *Job 1.21*

Let us pray:

O God, who shaped life
in the darkness of the earth's womb,
and called it forth
from the depths of the seas
and the moisture of the soil,
we look to you as the Holy Source of light and life,
shining ever-new day and night
and bringing forth light
even from earth's deepest darknesses
and human sorrows.
Whether we live in the midst
of births and new beginnings
or face endings
and the return to the ground that awaits us all,
we ask to see more light, O God,
in both our living and our dying.
From evils that haunt the world
and move threateningly among earth's people,
deliver us.
Renew us in the wisdom
that withstands every attempt
to hold life in bondage,
for we would be free, O God.

**Holy God,
holy and mighty,**

holy and immortal,
have mercy upon us.

A HYMN *may be sung*

PSALM

THE FIRST READING (*from the Old Testament*)

SILENCE *may be kept*

CANTICLE
A SONG OF THE CREATOR

Where were you when I laid the foundation of the earth?
And who determined its measurements?
Or who shut in the sea with doors
when it burst out from the womb –
and said, 'Thus far shall you come, and no farther,
and here shall your proud waves be stopped'?
Have you commanded the morning since your days began,
and caused the dawn to know its place?
Have the gates of death been revealed to you,
or have you seen the gates of deep darkness
or the way to the dwelling of light?
And who has put wisdom in the inward parts,
or given understanding to the human mind?
Tell me, if you have understanding.
Job 38

THE SECOND READING (*from the New Testament*)

SILENCE *may be kept*

A SERMON *may be preached*

PRAYERS OF THANKSGIVING AND INTERCESSION
We give thanks, O God,
for every blessing in life,
for the gifts of the past
and our memories of all that has been good:
for the times of well-being and security
when we have been held in the love and shelter
of family and friends;
for moments of happiness and generosity
when food and drink and human company
have been shared and delighted in.
And as we remember in gratitude these things,
we pray for people everywhere
who are in the midst of what will be remembered
not as good but as testing times,
painful or empty or terrifying:
for people who are experiencing
what they have most feared or dreaded,
the loss of a loved one,
the ending of a relationship,
the discovery of illness;
and for those who know no safe place,
who are troubled within themselves
or frightened by hostilities around them.
With men and women throughout the world
we pray your safeguarding and deliverance, O God,
of innocent ones and those unjustly wronged.
For all who are afflicted and struggling this night, *today*
we ask your comfort, dear God.
[*Here free prayer may be offered.*]

THE LORD'S PRAYER
Lord, teach us to pray together:

Our Father . . .

A HYMN may be sung

CANTICLE
A SONG OF HEALING

To this you have been called,
because Christ suffered for you, leaving you an example,
so that you should follow in his steps.
He committed no sin, and no deceit was found in his mouth.
When he was abused, he did not return abuse;
when he suffered, he did not threaten,
but entrusted himself to the One who judges justly.
He carried up our sins in his body to the tree,
so that, free from sin, we might live for righteousness.
By his wounds we have been healed.
1 Peter 2

CLOSING PRAYER
O God, who speaks in many and diverse ways,
in the glory of creation
and the ancient wisdom of Scripture,
in the words and actions of men and women
and the dreams and thoughts of the night,
assure us in all these things of your love,
so that when we are shaken,
or in an instant lose what is precious to us,
we may know that you are the Redeemer
of our lives and of all life,
and that at the last
your salvation will be known on earth.

BENEDICTION

DAY FOUR
The Prophet Jeremiah
Morning Prayer

'When you search for me, you will find me', says the Lord, 'if you seek me with all your heart.' *Jeremiah 29.13*

Let us pray:

With our whole heart
we return to you, O God,
not that you have ever been absent from us
but that often we have been absent
from our true selves
and therefore from you
at the centre of life.
You knew us and cherished us
even before our bodies were formed,
and consecrated us to life
even before we were born.
You surround us
and pour life upon us
in the light of the morning sun
and in the brightness of the moon at night.
Here in this set-apart place
we pause to listen
before running with the busyness of our days.
Here we gather
to receive again your promise
that when we call
you will hear,
and that when we confess our wrongdoings

you will forgive us
and remember our sin no more.

Lord have mercy upon us.
Christ have mercy upon us.
Lord have mercy upon us.

A HYMN may be sung

PSALM

THE FIRST READING (*from the Old Testament*)

SILENCE may be kept

CANTICLE
A SONG OF JOY

I have loved you with an everlasting love,
therefore I have continued my faithfulness to you.
Hear the word of the Lord, O nations,
and declare it in the coastlands far away.
For the Lord has ransomed Jacob,
and has redeemed him from hands too strong for him.
They shall come and sing aloud on the height of Zion,
and they shall be radiant over the goodness of the Lord.
Their life shall become like a watered garden,
and they shall never languish again.
Then shall the young women rejoice in the dance,
and the young men and the old shall be merry.
I will turn their mourning into joy,
I will comfort them and give them gladness for sorrow.
Jeremiah 31

THE SECOND READING (*from the New Testament*)

SILENCE may be kept

A SERMON may be preached

PRAYERS OF THANKSGIVING AND INTERCESSION
Blessed are you, O God,
for the gift of life,
and for the silence at the heart of creation
from which sounds of joy and gladness come forth:
for the song of early dawn,
birds waking and calling life from sleep;
and for the wind moving over the waters,
stirring the sea into sound.
We give thanks for the human voice of gladness,
of children's mirth and laughter,
of songs of remembrance and celebration
that come forth from the security of peace,
and for tender tones of affection
that issue from love's inner contentment.
And as we give thanks for the gift of life
and for the sounds that signal its goodness,
we pray for those places
within our world and our lives
where joy and gladness are not heard:
for cities that lie in ruins
and war-torn people and nations,
for men and women and families
held captive physically or emotionally
and barred from their homes and countries
or denied the liberties of expression and movement,
and for those who are weary
or weakened by troubles
and those who are dying and frightened.
For all people,
for our loved ones and ourselves,
we pray,
asking that more and more
we may know your stillness within us, O God,

and that our lives
may give voice to joy and gladness.
[*Here free prayer may be offered.*]

THE LORD'S PRAYER
Lord, teach us to pray together:

Our Father . . .

A HYMN may be sung

CANTICLE
A SONG OF PRAISE

I will sing to my God a new song:
you are great and glorious, O Lord,
wonderful in strength and invincible.
Let all your creatures serve you,
for you spoke and they were made.
You sent forth your spirit, and it formed them;
there is none that can resist your voice.
For the mountains shall be shaken to their foundations
with the waters;
and the rocks shall melt like wax.
But to those who fear you you show mercy;
and whoever fears you is great for ever.
Judith 16

CLOSING PRAYER
That health may be restored in and among us,
that the ways of life and goodness
may still be chosen
and the paths of death and destructiveness denounced,
these things lead us, O God,
to look faithfully to the road ahead.
Open our eyes

that we may see the ever-new thing
that you have prepared for us
and for all people;
open our hearts
that we may know within us your promise
that wherever we are
and whatever we have done
there is hope for the future.

BENEDICTION

The Prophet Jeremiah
Evening Prayer

OPENING SENTENCE AND PRAYER
'Call to me and I will answer you,' says the Lord, 'and will tell
you great and hidden things that you have not known.'
Jeremiah 33.3

Let us pray:

Within us, O God,
we find the fountain of your living waters
and endless fields of delight and goodness
prepared by you for our health and strength;
yet the wrongs of the world and of our lives
reach deep into our very hearts
and close off for us
the ways that lead to your life-springs,
leaving parts of us in exile from you.
In your mercy, open again
the paths that you have established within us

40

which lead to your dwelling
so that once more we may find rest for our souls
and again learn truths hidden from outward sight
but written for us and all people in the inner heart.
It is for a replenishing of strength,
a restoring of health
that we pray,
in the firm belief
that a healing of our spirits
is for the healing also of our families,
of our nations and world, O God.

Holy God,
holy and mighty,
holy and immortal,
have mercy upon us.

A HYMN *may be sung*

PSALM

THE FIRST READING (*from the Old Testament*)

SILENCE *may be kept*

CANTICLE
A SONG OF TRUST

Blessed are those who trust in the Lord,
whose trust is the Lord.
They shall be like a tree planted by water,
sending out its roots by the stream.
It shall not fear when heat comes,
and its leaves shall stay green.
In the year of drought it is not anxious,
and it does not cease to bear fruit.
Heal me, O Lord, and I shall be healed;

save me, and I shall be saved;
for you are my praise.
Jeremiah 17

THE SECOND READING (*from the New Testament*)

SILENCE *may be kept*

A SERMON *may be preached*

PRAYERS OF THANKSGIVING AND INTERCESSION
O God,
who is in the midst of us
and does not forsake us,
who has loved us from the beginning
and will love us to the end,
we give thanks
for the gifts of life that we have received:
for children born of us,
for the health and strength of body and mind
that have been ours,
and for the times when we have been saved
suffering and from trouble.
And in offering thanks
for the goodness that has come our way
and the new beginnings that have been given us
out of endings and failures and disappointments,
we pray for those whose pains seem unceasing
and whose wounds appear incurable:
for nations caught in conflicts
that are multiplied and deepened with time and memory;
for women and men and children
who suffer from torn and embittered relationships;
and for those
whose minds and souls are scarred
by past rejection and cruelty.
For all who are in need

and who cry out in the pain of struggle and labour,
but have no real hope
for new life born from their sufferings,
we offer prayer, O God,
in the hope that you will be their refuge
and ours
in the time of trouble.
[*Here free prayer may be offered.*]

THE LORD'S PRAYER
Lord, teach us to pray together:

Our Father . . .

A HYMN *may be sung*

CANTICLE
A SONG OF PROMISE

I will sprinkle clean water upon you,
and you shall be clean from all your uncleannesses.
A new heart I will give you,
and a new spirit I will put within you.
I will remove from your body the heart of stone
and give you a heart of flesh.
I will put my spirit within you,
that you may follow my ways.
Then you shall be my people,
and I will be your God.
Ezekiel 36

CLOSING PRAYER
Let us never forget
who we are,
from whom we have come,
and to whom we are called.
And on the journey of return

let us seek truth together
and act justly,
being alert to the cause of the poor
and defending the rights of those in need.
In all of this, O God,
set us free
from clinging insecurely
to things and people and places,
so that the liberty we proclaim for all
may be the liberty we know in our hearts.

BENEDICTION

DAY FIVE
Ecclesiasticus
Morning Prayer

OPENING SENTENCE AND PRAYER
God lifts up the soul and makes the eyes sparkle; he gives
health and life and blessing. *Ecclesiasticus 34.16*

Let us pray:

O God of all life,
whose wisdom in the beginning
fashioned the body and soul of each creature,
and filled the earth, the sea and skies
with good things
and with living beings of every kind,
we wonder at your limitless creativity
ever new,
inexhaustibly calling forth life.
Here we gather to reflect on the mystery
of all things interwoven with your life.
Here we seek the root of peace and well-being
for ourselves and for our world,
and turn to the hidden wisdom
that was born with us in the womb,
given for every people
and for the whole of creation.
Here we again direct our souls to you, O God,
for we believe that your Holy Wisdom is close to us
and is shown to the humble in heart.

Lord have mercy upon us.
Christ have mercy upon us.
Lord have mercy upon us.

Morning and Evening Prayer

A HYMN *may be sung*

PSALM

THE FIRST READING (*from the Old Testament*)

SILENCE *may be kept*

CANTICLE
A SONG OF THE WISE

Happy is the person who meditates on wisdom,
who reflects in his heart on her ways and ponders her secrets.
For she will come to meet him like a mother,
and like a young bride she will welcome him.
She will feed him with the bread of learning,
and give him the water of wisdom to drink.
He will lean on her and not fall,
and he will rely on her and not be put to shame.
Ecclesiasticus 14–15

THE SECOND READING (*from the New Testament*)

SILENCE *may be kept*

A SERMON *may be preached*

PRAYERS OF THANKSGIVING AND INTERCESSION
We give thanks, O God,
for the gift of life,
for the soul of every living thing
coming forth from your Soul,
and the form of every creature
issuing forth from the earth.
We give thanks for the great tree of life,
branched and spreading throughout creation,
for its strength and rootedness

and its fresh buddings of life.
We offer thanks for those who have gone before,
and through whom life has flowed to us,
for those from whom we have received,
whose understanding and wisdom
and acts of love and kindness
still live among us
in our memories of them.
We give thanks
for those among whom we have lived and loved,
for the delight and shelter of their friendship,
and for the moments of joy
that have opened and expanded life for us.
Free us and all people
from the divisions and jealousies
that impoverish and destroy life.
We pray for those caught in bitterness of spirit,
for whole communities trapped
in the things of anger and strife,
for those who have been betrayed or left behind,
whose hearts are filled with feelings of loss
and fears of the unknown,
and who long for comfort and peace
in the midst of their troubles and unrest.
And as we remember in the great flow of life
the passing of previous generations,
the ones we have honoured and held dear
who now are beyond our earthly sight,
we turn our thoughts also
to those who come after us in life's journey,
to our children
and to the newly born in every place,
and pray for the future that is theirs.
[*Here free prayer may be offered.*]

THE LORD'S PRAYER
Lord, teach us to pray together:

Our Father . . .

A HYMN may be sung

CANTICLE
A SONG OF GUIDANCE

With all your soul fear the Lord;
with all your might love your Maker.
And stretch out your hand to the poor,
so that your blessing may be complete.
Give graciously to all the living;
do not withhold kindness even from the dead.
Do not avoid those who weep,
but mourn with those who mourn.
Do not hesitate to visit the sick,
because for such deeds you will be loved.
In all you do, remember the end of your life,
that you may be free from sin.
Ecclesiasticus 7

CLOSING PRAYER
In our daily lives, O God,
grant us the discernment
to seek what is good
and to beware of evil.
Inspire us to choose life
and to turn from destructive thought and action.
Teach us to overlook one another's faults
that we may judge as we would hope to be judged,
and to grow in a true love for ourselves
that we may learn to be generous to others.
Open our souls to you in all things
and to the soul of every living creature

both to receive and to give,
and in giving
to be confident of what we have to offer,
for you are our maker, O God.

BENEDICTION

Ecclesiasticus
Evening Prayer

OPENING SENTENCE AND PRAYER
Trust in God, and he will help you; make your ways straight,
and hope in him. *Ecclesiasticus 2.6*

Let us pray:

We wait for you, O God,
and for your mercy,
for we believe that your compassion
is for every living thing.
May we not be ashamed to confess our sin
nor be so proud as to forget our need
and withdraw our hearts from you, our Maker.
O Holy One,
who searches out the depths of the human spirit
and knows our innermost thoughts,
here may we forgive that we may receive forgiveness,
here may we let go of resentment towards others
that we may seek pardon for ourselves.
Here may we leave behind us
the busyness of our lives
that we may undistractedly seek the change of heart
that will change the way we live.
Here, O God, we return to choose life and goodness

and to turn from the things that darken our souls.
Here we hope for new beginnings
and for inner peace and well-being.
Lead us, O God,
into the light of health once again.

**Holy God,
holy and mighty,
holy and immortal,
have mercy upon us.**

A HYMN *may be sung*

PSALM

THE FIRST READING *(from the Old Testament)*

SILENCE *may be kept*

CANTICLE
A SONG OF GOD'S IMAGE

The Lord created human beings out of earth,
and makes them return to it again.
**He endowed them with strength like his own,
and made them in his own image**.
He filled them with knowledge and understanding,
and showed them good and evil.
**He bestowed knowledge upon them,
and allotted to them the law of life.**
He established with them an eternal covenant,
and revealed to them his decrees.
**And their eyes saw his glorious majesty,
and their ears heard the glory of his voice.**
Ecclesiasticus 17

THE SECOND READING *(from the New Testament)*

SILENCE *may be kept*

A SERMON *may be preached*

PRAYERS OF THANKSGIVING AND INTERCESSION
Blessed are you, O God,
for you have filled the temple of creation
with a glory of life that glows.
We bless you for the light of the sun
and the moon and the stars,
for the whiteness of mountain snow
and the glistening of waters.
We give thanks for the goodness
that grows from the ground,
and from which health and wholeness come.
And in remembering with thanks
the times and places
of plenty and well-being in our lives,
we stand also in prayer
with those who are denied these things,
and ask that they not be forsaken
in their time of trouble.
Let the cry of the poor be heard, O God,
in heaven and on earth,
let the needy not be kept waiting,
let the hungry be fed,
and let the oppressed be set free.
For these and all who long for freedom
and for healing in body and soul
we offer prayer, O God.
[*Here free prayer may be offered.*]

THE LORD'S PRAYER
Lord, teach us to pray together:

Our Father . . .

A HYMN *may be sung*

CANTICLE
A SONG TO GOD

And now bless the God of all, who
everywhere works great wonders,
who fosters our growth from birth,
and deals with us according to his mercy.
May he give us gladness of heart, and
may there be peace as in days of old.
May he entrust to us his mercy and
deliver us in our days.
Ecclesiasticus 50

CLOSING PRAYER
With all our soul
inspire us to seek wisdom, O God,
that in loving her
we may more and more love life.
Lead us into the company of wise men and women
that we may receive of their spiritual treasure
as well as from the counsel of our own hearts.
Grant us the patience
to grow together in understanding,
so that the peace and wholeness that wisdom brings
may be known among us.
And may we be so guided by your inner light, O God,
that no darkness may overwhelm us,
neither the frightening darknesses
of earth and its sorrows
nor the sleep of eternity
that waits to restore us all.

BENEDICTION

DAY SIX
The Prophet Hosea
Morning Prayer

OPENING SENTENCE AND PRAYER
Seek the Lord, that he may come and rain righteousness upon you. *Hosea 10.12*

Let us pray:

Glory be to you, O God of all creation,
ever steadfast in your love,
guiding, forgiving, healing,
true to our mothers and fathers,
and faithful to us
even when we have been least aware.
Your love, O God,
is as constant as the rising sun.
To you we look in the morning light.
Forgive our wrongdoings,
heal our disloyalties,
renew the goodness that is planted within us,
and transform our shame
into a new sense of life's glory,
that we may love you
and one another once again.

Lord have mercy upon us.
Christ have mercy upon us.
Lord have mercy upon us.

A HYMN *may be sung*

PSALM

THE FIRST READING (*from the Old Testament*)

SILENCE *may be kept*

CANTICLE
A SONG OF RENEWAL

'Come, let us return to the Lord;
for it is he who has torn, and he will heal us;
he has struck down, and he will bind us up.
After two days he will revive us;
on the third day he will raise us up,
that we may live before him.
Let us know, let us press on to know the Lord;
his appearing is as sure as the dawn.
And he will come to us like the showers,
like the spring rains that water the earth.'
Hosea 6

THE SECOND READING (*from the New Testament*)

SILENCE *may be kept*

A SERMON *may be preached*

PRAYERS OF THANKSGIVING AND INTERCESSION
O God of all faithfulness, God of all goodness,
who delights in the loyalties of men and women,
of brother and sister,
parent and child,
yet whose faithfulness is not limited to blood and race,
but extends to all people and all time,
we offer thanks for the signs of constancy
that are all around us:
for mothers who labour in birth
and hold their children
close to their hearts throughout life;

for the simple kindliness of neighbours,
unassuming and freely given;
and for the testing times
when we have been given strength
to be true to ourselves
and to our hopes and commitments.
All faithfulness flows from you, O God,
like a river running through the whole of the universe,
in the unerring movement of the planets above,
and below in the abounding fertility of the earth.
And yet we know also the dark streaks of unfaithfulness
that run through all things,
of earth's elements in disturbed imbalances,
of oppression and suffering inflicted,
of bloodshed following bloodshed,
and indifference multiplying indifference.
And so it is our concern for the world,
as well as the hurts and struggles of our own lives,
which we bring in prayer to you,
O Healer of the wounded.
[*Here free prayer may be offered.*]

THE LORD'S PRAYER
Lord, teach us to pray together:

Our Father . . .

A HYMN *may be sung*

CANTICLE
THE SONG OF HANNAH

'My heart exults in the Lord;
and my strength is found in him.
**There is no Holy One like the Lord;
there is no Rock like our God.**
The Lord is a God of knowledge,

and by him actions are weighed.
The bows of the mighty are broken,
but the feeble gird on strength.
Those who were full have hired themselves out for bread,
but those who were hungry are filled.
The barren woman bears sevenfold,
but the mother of many is forlorn.
The Lord gives life and takes it away;
he brings down to the grave and raises up.
He lifts the poor from the dust,
and gives them a place with princes.
He guards the feet of the faithful,
but the wicked shall vanish in darkness;
for not by might does one prevail.'
1 Samuel 2

CLOSING PRAYER
May our morning awareness of you, O God,
endure more than the mist that scatters early in the day,
and as you have been our God from the beginning of time
may we be your faithful people
in the living of our lives together.
Grant us a new depth of seeing
so that the mystery of your presence in each thing
may not seem strange to us,
but rather be the light by which we are guided;
and may the divine foolishness of saints before us
and their openness to the promptings of the Spirit
be our wisdom and our way.

BENEDICTION

The Prophet Hosea
Evening Prayer

OPENING SENTENCE AND PRAYER
Return to your God, hold fast to love and justice, and wait
continually for him. *Hosea 12.6*

Let us pray:

Speak tenderly to us this night, O God,
speak tenderly
in the words of Scripture,
in the stillness of our hearts,
and in the quiet of this place,
for it is in these utterings of love
that what is torn in us may be healed,
and what is broken between us
may be made whole again.
O Holy One at the heart of life,
if we choose not to uncover our inner selves to you,
where else shall we turn in hope,
for there are wildernesses within,
parched places between and all around us
that only your life-giving springs can touch.
And so it is to you, O God,
that we call,
not only with our lips
but with our hearts' desires.

Holy God,
holy and mighty,
holy and immortal,
have mercy upon us.

A HYMN may be sung

PSALM

THE FIRST READING (*from the Old Testament*)

SILENCE may be kept

CANTICLE
A SONG OF NEW BEGINNINGS

I will heal their disloyalty;
I will love them freely, says the Lord,
for my anger has turned from them.
I will be like the dew to Israel;
he shall blossom like the lily,
he shall strike root like a great forest.
They shall again live beneath my shadow,
they shall flourish like a garden.
They shall blossom like the vine,
their fragrance shall be like the wine of Lebanon.
Hosea 14

THE SECOND READING (*from the New Testament*)

SILENCE may be kept

A SERMON may be preached

PRAYERS OF THANKSGIVING AND INTERCESSION
Blessed are you, O God,
giver of all that grows from the ground,
maker of every creature that flies in the air
and every life form that swarms the seas.
Blessed are you,
ever creating in the heights and depths,
for riches beneath the earth's surface,
and the thoughts and creativities
that wait within us to be brought to light,

for the expanding universe above and all around,
and the imagination ever opening,
for ocean depths still to be explored,
and the treasures of the unconscious
that well up from within us.
In all of this, O God,
we wonder at the limitless unfolding
of your gift of life.
And yet we know also within and among us
the contractions of death and disease,
and as lands go barren
and creatures perish,
so men and women and whole communities
are broken in body and soul.
It is these concerns
that we bring in prayer before you, O God,
yearning for the day you have promised,
of peace between heaven and earth
and between earth and all her people.
[*Here free prayer may be offered.*]

THE LORD'S PRAYER
Lord, teach us to pray together:

Our Father . . .

A HYMN *may be sung*

CANTICLE
A SONG OF REJOICING

Alleluia. Salvation and glory and power belong to God,
for his judgements are true and just
Praise him, all you servants of the Lord,
you who fear him, both great and small.
Alleluia. For the home of God is among mortals.
He will dwell with them as their God,

and they will be his people.
He will wipe every tear from their eyes,
for death will be no more.
Mourning and crying and pain will be no more.
Amen Alleluia.
Revelation 19–21

CLOSING PRAYER
Not only in moments of prayer, O God,
but in the ordinary hours of our days,
may seeds of your Spirit
come to life within the soil of our lives.
From heaven, rain down your life-giving waters
that we may be vibrant in love and faithfulness,
and that between us and among us as people and nations,
we may reap the fruits of justice and kindness together.

BENEDICTION

DAY SEVEN
The Song of Songs
Morning Prayer

OPENING SENTENCE AND PRAYER
Set me as a seal upon your heart, as a seal upon your arm; for love is strong as death. *Song of Songs 8.6*

Let us pray:

Visit us with your love in the morning, O God,
and we shall be satisfied,
for your love is better than wine
and your presence is like scented oil poured out.
O you, whom our souls love,
often we have sought but not found you;
we have listened but not heard.
Let us see your face in the day's glory of light,
and let us hear your voice
in the morning song of all that lives,
for your voice is beautiful,
and your face is radiant.
O you, who dwell in the garden of creation,
our hearts are awakened
by the stirrings of your Spirit among us.

Lord have mercy upon us.
Christ have mercy upon us.
Lord have mercy upon us.

A HYMN *may be sung*

PSALM

THE FIRST READING (*from the Old Testament*)

SILENCE may be kept

CANTICLE
A SONG OF CREATION

Bless the Lord, all you works of the Lord;
sing praise to him and highly exalt him for ever.
**Bless the Lord, you angels of light
and all heavenly powers of the Lord.**
Bless the Lord, sun and moon,
nights and days, all light and darkness;
sing praise to him and highly exalt him for ever.
**Let the earth bless the Lord,
mountains and hills, and all that grows from the ground.**
Bless the Lord, seas and rivers,
you whales and all that swim in the waters;
sing praise to him and highly exalt him for ever.
**Bless the Lord, every bird of the air,
all wild animals and cattle.**
Bless the Lord, all people on earth
and you who are holy and humble in heart;
sing praise to him and highly exalt him for ever.
Daniel 3 (Apocrypha)

THE SECOND READING (*from the New Testament*)

SILENCE may be kept

A SERMON may be preached

PRAYERS OF THANKSGIVING AND INTERCESSION
Blessed are you, O God of all creation,
for the goodness of the earth,
for its blossoming and season of bearing fruit,
for its colours and forms returning to the ground

and for its time of rest.
Blessed are you
for the cycles of dying and birth,
for the rhythms of darkness and light.
In the heights and depths of creation we know you,
in the mountains and glens,
in the stars and deep salt seas,
in the inspired visions of the human imagination
and in the awakened senses of the body.
Each thing that you have created
has a brightness of glory in it,
each human spirit made to shine like the dawn.
And yet in the midst of this glory and goodness
we know also forces of destruction
within and around us.
And so for the world and for ourselves
we offer prayer, O God.
[*Here free prayer may be offered.*]

THE LORD'S PRAYER
Lord, teach us to pray together:

Our Father . . .

A HYMN may be sung

CANTICLE
A SONG OF WISDOM

'O God of my ancestors and Lord of mercy,
who have called all things into being,
and by wisdom have formed humankind
to rule the world in righteousness,
grant me the wisdom that sits by your throne,
for she knows your works
and was present when you made the world.
She understands what is pleasing in your sight

and what is right according to your commandments.
Send her forth from the holy heavens,
and from the throne of your glory send her,
that she may labour at my side,
and that I may learn what is pleasing to you.
For she knows and understands all things,
and will guide me wisely and guard me with her glory.'
Wisdom 9

CLOSING PRAYER
Seal our hearts with your love, O God,
with a passion stronger than death.
Let us know within our souls
the fire of life that is inextinguishable,
and draw us after you
to places of both joy and struggle in the world,
there to know that all are yours and you are ours,
and that your desire is for every living thing.
There we will give you our love.

BENEDICTION

The Song of Songs
Evening Prayer

OPENING SENTENCE AND PRAYER
Many waters cannot quench love, neither can floods drown it.
Song of Songs 8.7

Let us pray:

O you, who awakened us to life,
who knew us before our mothers bore us
and loved us in the labour of birth;

as you shone with kindness in the morning light
so enfold us in the darkness of evening;
as you watched with love at the beginning of our days
so hold us when days are past.
From early till late,
from the first to the last,
amidst our living and in our dying,
your intention towards us is love.
Guide us this night in the things of the eternal;
lead us with your Spirit,
and let us taste of the fruits that are forever,
O you, whom our souls love.

Holy God,
holy and mighty,
holy and immortal,
have mercy upon us.

A HYMN *may be sung*

PSALM

THE FIRST READING (*from the Old Testament*)

SILENCE *may be kept*

CANTICLE
A SONG OF FORGIVENESS

Remember these things, O Jacob,
for you are my servant.
I formed you, O Israel,
and you will not be forgotten by me.
I have swept away your transgressions like a cloud,
and your sins like a mist.
Return to me, for I have redeemed you.
Sing, O heavens, for the Lord has done it.

**Shout, O depths of the earth,
and break forth into singing.**
Isaiah 44

THE SECOND READING (*from the New Testament*)

SILENCE may be kept

A SERMON *may be preached*

PRAYERS OF THANKSGIVING AND INTERCESSION
We give thanks, O God,
that all things are yours,
from the beginning to the end,
from the rising of the sun to its setting,
the solid rocks of the earth around us,
all that is vibrant with life,
all that flies above and swims in the seas.
And we too are yours,
the whole of our beings,
all that is seen and unseen in us,
all that is known and still to be known.
We give thanks
that your Spirit is deep within the human spirit,
that the life of heaven
is interwoven among the things of earth,
and that the hope of what is yet to be
has been placed within us.
For your unending stream of life, O God,
that flows through the whole of creation,
we give you thanks.
Unlock the garden that is each of us,
unseal the fountain of the waters that will never fail,
that we may be made new again.
[*Here free prayer may be offered.*]

THE LORD'S PRAYER
Lord, teach us to pray together:

Our Father . . .

A HYMN may be sung

CANTICLE
THE SONG OF MARY

My soul magnifies the Lord,
and my spirit rejoices in God my Saviour;
**for he has looked with favour on the lowliness of
his servant;**
from this day all generations will call me blessed;
for the Mighty One has done great things for me,
and holy is his name.
**His mercy is for those who fear him
from generation to generation.**
He has shown strength with his arm;
he has scattered the proud in the thoughts of their hearts.
**He has brought down the powerful from their thrones,
and lifted up the lowly.**
He has filled the hungry with good things,
and sent the rich away empty.
**He has helped his servant Israel,
in remembrance of his mercy,**
according to the promise he made to our ancestors,
to Abraham and to his descendants for ever.
Luke 1

CLOSING PRAYER
May we ever know your presence among us, O God.
Free us from dividing the holy from the ordinary,
lest we think that you visit us
only in the set apart place and time,
lest we think that it is only here

that we open the doors of our hearts to you.
In all places, in all times,
in all the people whom we meet,
your presence is round us
and we look with expectation.
Even in sleep may our hearts be awake to you,
in our dreams and subconscious depths.
O Lover of our ever-living souls,
watch over us and all creation this night.
Until the day breathes and the shadows of night flee,
assure us, O God, of your world-encompassing love.

BENEDICTION

Part Two

COMMUNION
LITURGIES

INTRODUCTION

These seven liturgies, each inspired by a writer in the New Testament, provide a wide spectrum of language and imagery for celebrating communion. The liturgy for Day One, for instance, draws on the words and thought of St John's Gospel: the themes of the Word that was in the beginning calling creation into being and of the light that enlightens every person. Day Two reflects the writings of St Peter: his vision of God as the Guardian of our ever-living souls, and of Christ being wounded so that the world may be healed. The liturgy of St Paul on Day Three uses imagery of the One from whom and to whom are all things, of Christ in his battle against powers of darkness, and of our inclusion into the heights and depths of the mystery. The liturgy for Day Four employs St James' passion for justice and the cry of the poor, accentuating God's generosity and seeing Christ as the perfect gift given from above. The liturgy for Day Five is based on St Luke's Gospel: his conviction of God's strength and tenderness enduring over the ages to lift up the lowly and to scatter the proud, and of the Son of Mary bringing wholeness through the forgiveness of sins. Day Six and the liturgy of the Apostle to the Hebrews focuses on heaven and earth as having come forth from the invisible realm of spirit, Christ abiding forever in the inner sanctuary of life, and the assurance that is planted within us of things not yet seen. The final liturgy draws on the imagery of St John the Divine: his revelation of God as the beginning and the end, and the ultimate hope for the healing of the nations.

The opening preparation and the liturgy of the word in these services are much like those of the daily office, with the addition of the traditional prayer for purity and the inclusion of the Matthew 22 passage as a constant reminder of the imperative to love God above all else and to love our neighbour as ourself. There is a variety of lectionaries to choose from among the churches. One for daily communion, designed to supplement the 'Sundays and Seasons' communion lectionary, can be found in *The Alternative Service Book 1980*. This essentially follows the pattern of daily readings in the Roman Catholic *Weekday Missal* and *Sunday Missal*, the main difference being that the missal lections are printed out in full.

The liturgy of the sacrament in this book is modelled on the basic structure of eucharistic prayer in some of the oldest liturgical texts of the Church, namely those preserved in the *Apostolic Tradition* of Hippolytus of Rome, written c.215, and the fourth-century Syrian document, the *Testament of our Lord Jesus Christ*. Although these seven communion liturgies have been written primarily in the context of worship within the Church of Scotland, they do not reflect the eucharistic structure of any one modern tradition so much as reflect a combination of early Church eucharistic structure and biblical imagery together with a new writing of prayer for today. Throughout the liturgies there is this mixture of the historic with the new. The words of the offertory prayer, for instance, are based on the ancient Jewish table prayer which Jesus would have used at the Last Supper. At a Jewish meal the head of the household would take bread and break it with the words 'Blessed are you, O Lord our God, eternal King, who brings forth bread from the earth'. And, similarly, when wine was served the words would be spoken, 'Blessed are you, O Lord our God, eternal King, who creates the fruit of the vine'.

And so the form of prayer used here at the offering of the elements draws on ancient tradition. Importantly it is a tradition that includes reference to creation and to the earth as part of what we offer for blessing. The second section of the offertory prayer, 'Receive these gifts . . .', is based on the Leonine Sacramentary, attributed to the fifth-century Bishop of Rome, Leo I.

There are a number of features in the liturgies of the early centuries which generally do not find their way into more recent eucharistic tradition, but which are followed here. One is the practice of dividing the initial thanksgiving prayer into two distinct sections, with the Sanctus and Benedictus separating them. This allows the Preface to be primarily a general ascription of glory to God and thanksgiving for creation. The second part of the thanksgiving then focuses specifically on redemption and the work of Christ and his saints and angels. The whole of the thanksgiving is written not with the sort of doctrinal precision that is found in most traditional eucharistic prayers, but rather with a variety of biblical imagery that provides a tapestry of ways of seeing the creative and redemptive work of God.

Another feature of the earlier liturgies which is here applied is that of placing the intercessory prayers (or the diptychs) in the midst of the eucharistic celebration rather than either before or after it. The emphasis is that in being renewed as members of Christ we are included in the mystery of his ever making intercession for the life of the world. This placing of the intercessions reminds us that our mystical communion with Christ is not a stepping away from the world but a moving more deeply into awareness of it and praying for its healing.

Like the morning and evening prayers the daily communion liturgies are set in a weekly pattern. Again this is not intended to restrict the use of a liturgy to once a week, for at certain times of the year one liturgy may be more suited than another to frequent use. During Advent, for example, the Liturgy of St John the Divine, with its theme of the coming of God, may be chosen, as might be the case during Holy Week in relation to the Liturgy of St Peter and its image of Christ wounded for the healing of the world. Also, certain parts of the liturgies will lend themselves to being inserted into other services on the basis of their themes. Prayers from the Liturgies of St James and St Luke, for example, can be introduced into services that are concentrating on the themes of justice and peace.

The setting in which a communion celebration occurs will significantly determine how music is to be made use of, or perhaps not made use of. Each of these communion liturgies has been employed in a whole variety of contexts, ranging from cathedral worship to simple gatherings of just two or three people. The liturgies may be adapted to a whole variety of settings, depending on the ways in which music, movement and silence are used.

PRAYERS BEFORE COMMUNION

As those who watch for the morning
so we watch for you, O Christ.
Come with the dawning of the day
and make yourself known to us
in the breaking of the bread.
A version of a traditional Christian prayer based on Psalm 130

Come, come, Lord Jesus,
and stand in our midst
as you did stand in the midst of your disciples,
and speak to us words of peace.
A version of a prayer from the Mozarabic Rite based on John 20

Come, O Christ,
and remain with us
for the day is ending.
Open our minds
that we may understand the Scriptures,
and our eyes
that we may recognize you among us.
A prayer based on Luke 24

DAY ONE
St John the Evangelist

THE PREPARATION

INTROIT Psalm

A HYMN *may be sung*

OPENING SENTENCE AND PRAYER
'Whoever follows me,' says Jesus, 'will never walk in darkness,
but will have the light of life.' *John 8.12*

Lord have mercy upon us.
Christ have mercy upon us.
Lord have mercy upon us.

Almighty God,
to whom all hearts are open,
all desires known,
and from whom no secrets are hidden:
cleanse the thoughts of our hearts
by the inspiration of your Holy Spirit,
that we may perfectly love you,
and worthily magnify your holy name;
through Jesus Christ our Lord.
Amen.

THE LITURGY OF THE WORD

SCRIPTURES

SILENCE *may be kept*

SUMMARY *of the Law may be read*
Jesus said, 'You shall love the Lord your God with all your
heart, and with all your soul, and with all your mind. This is
the greatest and first commandment. And the second is like it:
You shall love your neighbour as yourself.'
Matthew 22

REFLECTION/SERMON

THE LITURGY OF THE SACRAMENT

A HYMN may be sung

OFFERING
Blessed are you, O God of all creation,
through whose goodness we have this bread to offer,
which earth has given and human hands have made;
may it become for us the bread of life.

Blessed are you, O God of all creation,
through whose goodness we have this wine to offer,
fruit of the vine and work of human hands;
may it become for us the cup of blessing.

Receive these gifts, dear God,
and accept in them the sacrifice of ourselves.
In life and in death
may we be an offering to you for ever.

DIALOGUE
The Lord be with you.
And also with you.
Lift up your hearts.
We lift them to the Lord.
Let us give thanks to the Lord our God.
It is right to give him thanks and praise.

PREFACE TO THE THANKSGIVING
We offer you praise
and hearts lifted high, O God,
who called into being all that is,
and whose light enlightens every person
coming into the world.
Created good we know evil also,
yet you have not left us to death's powers
but offer us always hope for new life.
And so with the whole realm of nature around us,
with earth, sea and sky, we sing to you;
with angels of light who envelop us,
and with saints of heaven and of earth,
we join in the song of your unending greatness.

SANCTUS
Holy, holy, holy Lord,
God of power and might,
heaven and earth are full of your glory.
Hosanna in the highest.

BENEDICTUS
Blessed is he who comes
in the name of the Lord.
Hosanna in the highest.

THANKSGIVING FOR CHRIST
Holy in the heights of heaven,
holy in the depths of earth,
O God, your glory knows no bounds,
and your love is without end.
The Word that was in the beginning,
and through whom all things were made,
you sent to dwell among us,
full of grace and truth,
that believing in him
we may have springs of life within.

We bless you that in love for the world
your Son laid down his life,
and overcame death's powers
to be our hope of life everlasting;
that in love he poured out his Spirit
to lead us through encircling darknesses into all truth;
and that in love he returned to the Source of Light
to draw the earth and all its people to himself.

NARRATIVE
To the very end Jesus loved those whom he had been given,
and prayed that his love might be in them.
On the night when he was betrayed,
Jesus took bread,
and having blessed it,
he broke the bread,
and gave it to his disciples, saying:
'Take, eat.
This is my body which is broken for you.
This do in remembrance of me.'
In the same way he took wine,
and having given thanks for it,
he poured it out,
and gave the cup to his disciples, saying:
'This cup is the new covenant in my blood.
This do, as often as you drink it,
in remembrance of me.'

MEMORIAL PROCLAMATION
Remembering his eternal self-giving,
we proclaim the mystery of Christ among us.
Made one with him,
and thus one with each other,
we offer these gifts
and with them ourselves,
a single, holy living sacrifice.

INVOCATION
Hear us now, O Christ,
and breathe your Spirit upon us,
and upon this bread and this wine,
that they may be heaven's food and drink for us,
for you are the living bread
that comes down from heaven
to give life to the world;
you are the true vine
without whom we can do nothing.

INTERCESSIONS
In this mystery of communion with Christ,
let us remember with thanksgiving
those who have gone before us
and through whom life has flowed to us,
and with the whole company of saints
in heaven and on earth
let us be making our prayers of intercession
for the life of the world
[*here free prayer may be offered*]
through Christ.

DOXOLOGY
By whom,
with whom,
in whom,
in the unity of the Holy Spirit,
all glory and honour is yours, almighty God,
world without end.
Amen.

THE LORD'S PRAYER
Lord, teach us to pray together:

**Our Father in heaven,
hallowed be your name,**

your kingdom come,
your will be done,
on earth as in heaven.
Give us today our daily bread.
Forgive us our sins
as we forgive those who sin against us.
Lead us not into temptation
but deliver us from evil.
For the kingdom, the power,
and the glory are yours
now and for ever. Amen.

BREAKING OF THE BREAD
The bread of heaven
is broken
for the life of the world.

AGNUS DEI
Lamb of God,
who takes away the sin of the world:
have mercy upon us.
Lamb of God,
who takes away the sin of the world:
have mercy upon us.
Lamb of God,
who takes away the sin of the world:
grant us your peace.

COMMUNION

PEACE
The peace of the Lord Jesus Christ be with you. Let us greet
one another with a sign of peace.

THE SENDING OUT

CLOSING PRAYER
O Christ, who said to your disciples,
'Peace I leave with you,
my peace I give to you.
Not as the world gives do I give.'
Grant us and all people this peace,
guide us into truth,
and gather us into unity,
that we may love one another,
and that together we may know
that we are in you,
and you in God,
and God in us.
Amen.

A HYMN *may be sung*

DISMISSAL AND BENEDICTION
Go now in peace.
The grace of our Lord Jesus Christ,
the love of God,
and the communion of the Holy Spirit,
be with you.
Amen.

DAY TWO
St Peter the Apostle

THE PREPARATION

INTROIT Psalm

A HYMN *may be sung*

OPENING SENTENCE AND PRAYER
Cast all your anxiety on God, for he cares for you. *1 Peter 5.7*

Lord have mercy upon us.
Christ have mercy upon us.
Lord have mercy upon us.

Almighty God,
to whom all hearts are open,
all desires known,
and from whom no secrets are hidden:
cleanse the thoughts of our hearts
by the inspiration of your Holy Spirit,
that we may perfectly love you,
and worthily magnify your holy name;
through Jesus Christ our Lord.
Amen.

THE LITURGY OF THE WORD

SCRIPTURES

SILENCE *may be kept*

SUMMARY *of the Law may be read*
Jesus said, 'You shall love the Lord your God with all your
heart, and with all your soul, and with all your mind. This is
the greatest and first commandment. And the second is like it:
You shall love your neighbour as yourself.' *Matthew 22*

REFLECTION/SERMON

THE LITURGY OF THE SACRAMENT

A HYMN *may be sung*

OFFERING
Blessed are you, O God of all creation,
through whose goodness we have this bread to offer,
which earth has given and human hands have made;
may it become for us the bread of life.

Blessed are you, O God of all creation,
through whose goodness we have this wine to offer,
fruit of the vine and work of human hands;
may it become for us the cup of blessing.

Receive these gifts, dear God,
and accept in them the sacrifice of ourselves.
In life and in death
may we be an offering to you for ever.

DIALOGUE
The Lord be with you.
And also with you.
Lift up your hearts.
We lift them to the Lord.
Let us give thanks to the Lord our God.
It is right to give him thanks and praise.

PREFACE TO THE THANKSGIVING
We offer you praise
and hearts lifted high, O God,
by whose word the heavens were formed
and the earth was brought forth from the waters.
The reflection of your glory
shines in each created thing,
and, though earth's flowering fades,
you have planted within us imperishable seeds
for our salvation,
and call life out of death
into the light that endures forever.
And so with heaven and earth's host of light,
with the sainted women and men of every nation,
and with those who now live in the spirit
as you are Spirit,
we join in the song of your unending greatness.

SANCTUS
Holy, holy, holy Lord,
God of power and might,
heaven and earth are full of your glory.
Hosanna in the highest.

BENEDICTUS
Blessed is he who comes
in the name of the Lord.
Hosanna in the highest.

THANKSGIVING FOR CHRIST
Blessed are you, O God,
for the great day of salvation
prepared from the beginning of the world,
when Christ, though rejected on earth,
will be seen by all
to be chosen and precious in your sight.

We bless you for Christ
who carried in his body to the tree
sin's destructive powers
that we and all people might be set free.
Being put to death in the flesh
but made alive in the spirit,
and entering the captivity of hell
to liberate the imprisoned,
these things of Christ inspire the hope in us
that earth's forces of darkness will be scattered
and angels of glory and principalities of light
will bring a new heaven and a new earth.

NARRATIVE
Just as prophets long before Christ
had spoken of the sufferings that would be his,
so Jesus on the night when he was betrayed
took bread,
and having blessed it,
he broke the bread,
and gave it to his disciples, saying:
'Take, eat.
This is my body which is broken for you.
This do in remembrance of me.'
In the same way he took wine,
and having given thanks for it,
he poured it out,
and gave the cup to his disciples, saying:
'This cup is the new covenant in my blood.
This do, as often as you drink it,
in remembrance of me.'

MEMORIAL PROCLAMATION
Remembering his eternal self-giving,
we proclaim the mystery of Christ among us.
Made one with him,

and thus one with each other,
we offer these gifts
and with them ourselves,
a single, holy living sacrifice.

INVOCATION
Bless us with your Holy Spirit, O God,
and this bread and wine,
that through them we may be made strong again
with the strength that only you supply.
May our inner selves be nourished
that in the outward things of life
we may follow the way of Christ
and grow more and more into salvation.

INTERCESSIONS
In this mystery of communion with Christ,
let us remember with thanksgiving
those who have gone before us
and through whom life has flowed to us,
and with the whole company of saints
in heaven and on earth
let us be making our prayers of intercession
for the life of the world
[here free prayer may be offered]
through Christ.

DOXOLOGY
By whom,
with whom,
in whom,
in the unity of the Holy Spirit,
all glory and honour is yours, almighty God,
world without end.
Amen.

THE LORD'S PRAYER
Lord, teach us to pray together:

Our Father . . .

BREAKING OF THE BREAD
Christ is wounded
that the world may be healed.

AGNUS DEI
Lamb of God,
who takes away the sin of the world:
have mercy upon us.
Lamb of God,
who takes away the sin of the world:
have mercy upon us.
Lamb of God,
who takes away the sin of the world:
grant us your peace.

COMMUNION

PEACE
The peace of the Lord Jesus Christ be with you.
Let us greet one another with a sign of peace.

THE SENDING OUT

CLOSING PRAYER
Until the eternal day dawns
which Christ as morning star bore witness to,
may we catch sight
of the signs of glory all around us, O God.
And as in this set apart place
we have shared a mystery
into which angels long to look,

so in every place and every time
may we know the sacredness of life
and be servants of the holy in all things.
Strengthen us in the discipline of love
that we may live as free people,
generous and tenderhearted,
unbound by others' judgements and fears,
entrusting ourselves and all that is ours
to your safekeeping,
O Guardian of our ever-living souls.

A HYMN *may be sung*

DISMISSAL AND BENEDICTION
Go now in peace.
The grace of our Lord Jesus Christ,
the love of God,
and the communion of the Holy Spirit,
be with you.
Amen.

DAY THREE
St Paul the Apostle

THE PREPARATION

INTROIT Psalm

A HYMN may be sung

OPENING SENTENCE AND PRAYER
Eye has not seen, nor ear heard, neither has it entered the
human imagination, what God has prepared for those who
love him. *1 Corinthians 2.9*

Lord have mercy upon us.
Christ have mercy upon us.
Lord have mercy upon us.

Almighty God,
to whom all hearts are open,
all desires known,
and from whom no secrets are hidden:
cleanse the thoughts of our hearts
by the inspiration of your Holy Spirit,
that we may perfectly love you,
and worthily magnify your holy name;
through Jesus Christ our Lord.
Amen.

THE LITURGY OF THE WORD

SCRIPTURES

SILENCE may be kept

SUMMARY of the Law may be read
Jesus said, 'You shall love the Lord your God with all your
heart, and with all your soul, and with all your mind. This is
the greatest and first commandment. And the second is like it:
You shall love your neighbour as yourself.' *Matthew 22*

REFLECTION/SERMON

THE LITURGY OF THE SACRAMENT

A HYMN may be sung

OFFERING
Blessed are you, O God of all creation,
through whose goodness we have this bread to offer,
which earth has given and human hands have made;
may it become for us the bread of life.

Blessed are you, O God of all creation,
through whose goodness we have this wine to offer,
fruit of the vine and work of human hands;
may it become for us the cup of blessing.

Receive these gifts, dear God,
and accept in them the sacrifice of ourselves.
In life and in death
may we be an offering to you for ever.

DIALOGUE
The Lord be with you.
And also with you.
Lift up your hearts.
We lift them to the Lord.
Let us give thanks to the Lord our God.
It is right to give him thanks and praise.

PREFACE TO THE THANKSGIVING
We offer you praise
and hearts lifted high, O God,
whose blessing is seen
in the fullness of creation,
in the glory of the sun and moon,
in the goodness of the earth and its waters,
in your image deep within us.
Blessed are you,
from whom,
through whom,
and to whom are all things,
your mystery unfolding through the ages,
your Spirit yearning from within creation
for the earth's release from evil.
And so with angels and archangels,
and with the whole company of heaven,
we join in the song of your unending greatness.

SANCTUS
Holy, holy, holy Lord,
God of power and might,
heaven and earth are full of your glory.
Hosanna in the highest.

BENEDICTUS
Blessed is he who comes
in the name of the Lord.
Hosanna in the highest.

THANKSGIVING FOR CHRIST
Blessed are you, O God,
who in Christ has come
in the great struggle against powers of darkness
to reconcile all things,
things visible and invisible,
things of heaven and things of earth.

We bless you for Christ,
who died to free us from death's bondage,
and rose to lead us into life everlasting;
who imparted the Spirit of truth to us,
and ascended to be everywhere present
and to gather up all things
that at the last you may be all in all.

NARRATIVE
The tradition that comes down to us from the
Lord is that on the night when he was betrayed,
Jesus took bread,
and having blessed it,
he broke the bread,
and gave it to his disciples, saying:
'Take, eat.
This is my body which is broken for you.
This do in remembrance of me.'
In the same way he took wine,
and having given thanks for it,
he poured it out,
and gave the cup to his disciples, saying:
'This cup is the new covenant in my blood.
This do, as often as you drink it,
in remembrance of me.'

MEMORIAL PROCLAMATION
Remembering his eternal self-giving,
we proclaim the mystery of Christ among us.
Made one with him,
and thus one with each other,
we offer these gifts
and with them ourselves,
a single, holy living sacrifice.

INVOCATION
Bless us and these things
with your Holy Spirit, O God,
that the bread that we break
and the cup that we bless
may be a communion in Christ's body and blood,
and that we may be strengthened in our inner beings,
grounded again in love.

INTERCESSIONS
In this mystery of communion with Christ,
let us remember with thanksgiving
those who have gone before us
and through whom life has flowed to us,
and with the whole company of saints
in heaven and on earth
let us be making our prayers of intercession
for the life of the world
[*here free prayer may be offered*]
through Christ.

DOXOLOGY
By whom,
with whom,
in whom,
in the unity of the Holy Spirit,
all glory and honour is yours, almighty God,
world without end.
Amen.

THE LORD'S PRAYER
Lord, teach us to pray together:

Our Father . . .

BREAKING OF THE BREAD
The body of Christ
is broken
for the life of the world.

AGNUS DEI
Lamb of God,
who takes away the sin of the world:
have mercy upon us.
Lamb of God,
who takes away the sin of the world:
have mercy upon us.
Lamb of God,
who takes away the sin of the world:
grant us your peace.

COMMUNION

PEACE
The peace of the Lord Jesus Christ be with you.
Let us greet one another with a sign of peace.

THE SENDING OUT

CLOSING PRAYER
O Christ,
in whom is hidden
the wisdom and knowledge of God,
fill our minds
with everything that is true,
everything that is good,
and guide us by your Spirit
into the heights and the depths,
into the breadth and the length of the mystery,

that whether we live or whether we die,
we may know the love that surpasses knowledge,
and be signs of peace in the world.
Amen.

A HYMN *may be sung*

DISMISSAL AND BENEDICTION
Go now in peace.
The grace of our Lord Jesus Christ,
the love of God,
and the communion of the Holy Spirit,
be with you.
Amen.

DAY FOUR
St James the Just

THE PREPARATION

INTROIT Psalm

A HYMN *may be sung*

OPENING SENTENCE AND PRAYER
Draw near to God, and God will draw near to you. Humble
yourselves, and you will be raised up. *James 4.8, 10*

Lord have mercy upon us.
Christ have mercy upon us.
Lord have mercy upon us.

Almighty God,
to whom all hearts are open,
all desires known,
and from whom no secrets are hidden:
cleanse the thoughts of our hearts
by the inspiration of your Holy Spirit,
that we may perfectly love you,
and worthily magnify your holy name;
through Jesus Christ our Lord.
Amen.

THE LITURGY OF THE WORD

SCRIPTURES

SILENCE *may be kept*

SUMMARY *of the Law may be read*
Jesus said, 'You shall love the Lord your God with all your
heart, and with all your soul, and with all your mind. This is
the greatest and first commandment. And the second is like it:
You shall love your neighbour as yourself.' *Matthew 22*

REFLECTION/SERMON

THE LITURGY OF THE SACRAMENT

A HYMN *may be sung*

OFFERING
Blessed are you, O God of all creation,
through whose goodness we have this bread to offer,
which earth has given and human hands have made;
may it become for us the bread of life.

Blessed are you, O God of all creation,
through whose goodness we have this wine to offer,
fruit of the vine and work of human hands;
may it become for us the cup of blessing.

Receive these gifts, dear God,
and accept in them the sacrifice of ourselves.
In life and in death
may we be an offering to you for ever.

DIALOGUE
The Lord be with you.
And also with you.
Lift up your hearts.
We lift them to the Lord.
Let us give thanks to the Lord our God.
It is right to give him thanks and praise.

PREFACE TO THE THANKSGIVING
We offer you praise
and hearts lifted high, O God,
who as Father of lights
has given light and life to all that is.
Though our days vanish like mist,
and the form and shape of things disappear
like flowers in a field,
your Spirit is within all life
and every human soul is born in your likeness.
And so with the whole created order,
with the stars of the open skies
and all that glistens with life's glory,
with heaven's messengers of light
and with saints before and beside us,
we join in the song of your unending greatness.

SANCTUS
Holy, holy, holy Lord,
God of power and might,
heaven and earth are full of your glory.
Hosanna in the highest.

BENEDICTUS
Blessed is he who comes
in the name of the Lord.
Hosanna in the highest.

THANKSGIVING FOR CHRIST
Blessed are you, O God,
whose wisdom from above
has inspired men and women through the ages
to fulfil on earth your purposes,
to hear the cry of the poor,
to act with mercy
and to live together in gentleness and in peace.

We bless you for the coming of Christ,
who in life and in death
embodied the law of love,
and whose rising again and gift of the Holy Spirit
has implanted among us the hope
that saves the soul from death
and guides us in the conflict with evil
that rages around and within us.

NARRATIVE
It was in following the way of God's liberty
that Jesus chose to offer his life in love.
On the night when he was betrayed,
Jesus took bread,
and having blessed it,
he broke the bread,
and gave it to his disciples, saying:
'Take, eat.
This is my body which is broken for you.
This do in remembrance of me.'
In the same way he took wine,
and having given thanks for it,
he poured it out,
and gave the cup to his disciples, saying:
'This cup is the new covenant in my blood.
This do, as often as you drink it,
in remembrance of me.'

MEMORIAL PROCLAMATION
Remembering his eternal self-giving,
we proclaim the mystery of Christ among us.
Made one with him,
and thus one with each other,
we offer these gifts
and with them ourselves,
a single, holy living sacrifice.

INVOCATION
O God, whose generosity is unbounded
and who wills that we should lack no good thing,
bless this bread and this wine
with your Holy Spirit
that in receiving them into ourselves
we may be made whole again,
strengthened not merely to hear the truth
but to do it, and be blessed in our doing.

INTERCESSIONS
In this mystery of communion with Christ,
let us remember with thanksgiving
those who have gone before us
and through whom life has flowed to us,
and with the whole company of saints
in heaven and on earth
let us be making our prayers of intercession
for the life of the world
[*here free prayer may be offered*]
through Christ.

DOXOLOGY
By whom,
with whom,
in whom,
in the unity of the Holy Spirit,
all glory and honour is yours, almighty God,
world without end.
Amen.

THE LORD'S PRAYER
Lord, teach us to pray together:

Our Father . . .

BREAKING OF THE BREAD
The perfect gift from above
is given
for the life of the world.

AGNUS DEI
Lamb of God,
who takes away the sin of the world:
have mercy upon us.
Lamb of God,
who takes away the sin of the world:
have mercy upon us.
Lamb of God,
who takes away the sin of the world:
grant us your peace.

COMMUNION

PEACE
The peace of the Lord Jesus Christ be with you.
Let us greet one another with a sign of peace.

THE SENDING OUT

CLOSING PRAYER
O God,
who has bestowed earth's gifts
on all people,
free us from setting closed boundaries
on our giving and receiving.
Like the blessed bread and wine of this table
freely offered and equally shared
so may we generously give and openly receive
in our lives this day.

And on this and every day
grant us perseverance
like those who sow seeds in the ground
and wait patiently through sun and through rain.
So may we wait
for the fullness of your coming in all things,
O God.

A HYMN *may be sung*

DISMISSAL AND BENEDICTION
Go now in peace.
The grace of our Lord Jesus Christ,
the love of God,
and the communion of the Holy Spirit,
be with you.
Amen.

DAY FIVE
St Luke the Evangelist

THE PREPARATION

INTROIT Psalm

OPENING CONFESSION AND PRAYER
'Do not judge, and you will not be judged. Do not condemn,
and you will not be condemned. Forgive', says Jesus, 'and you
will be forgiven.' *Luke 6.37*

Lord have mercy upon us.
Christ have mercy upon us.
Lord have mercy upon us.

Almighty God,
to whom all hearts are open,
all desires known,
and from whom no secrets are hidden:
cleanse the thoughts of our hearts
by the inspiration of your Holy Spirit,
that we may perfectly love you,
and worthily magnify your holy name;
through Jesus Christ our Lord. Amen.

THE LITURGY OF THE WORD

SCRIPTURES

SILENCE *may be kept*

SUMMARY *of the Law may be read*
Jesus said, 'You shall love the Lord your God with all your
heart, and with all your soul, and with all your mind. This is
the greatest and first commandment. And the second is like it:
You shall love your neighbour as yourself.' *Matthew 22*

REFLECTION/SERMON

THE LITURGY OF THE SACRAMENT

A HYMN *may be sung*

OFFERING
Blessed are you, O God of all creation,
through whose goodness we have this bread to offer,
which earth has given and human hands have made;
may it become for us the bread of life.
    Blessed are you, O God of all creation,
through whose goodness we have this wine to offer,
fruit of the vine and work of human hands;
may it become for us the cup of blessing.
    Receive these gifts, dear God,
and accept in them the sacrifice of ourselves.
In life and in death
may we be an offering to you for ever.

DIALOGUE
The Lord be with you.
And also with you.
Lift up your hearts.
We lift them to the Lord.
Let us give thanks to the Lord our God.
It is right to give him thanks and praise.

PREFACE TO THE THANKSGIVING
We offer you praise
and hearts lifted high, O God,
by whose word the heavens and earth were formed
and the wind and waters of chaos subdued.
The grasses of the fields
you clothe in splendour,
the smallest creatures of the air
you cherish and adorn,
and from generation to generation
your strength and tender mercy have endured
to lift up the lowly
and to scatter the proud.
And so with heaven's glory that is in earth,
with ministering angels of light
whose message is peace
and with saints before us
who have died yet live,
we join in the song of your unending greatness.

SANCTUS
**Holy, holy, holy Lord,
God of power and might,
heaven and earth are full of your glory.
Hosanna in the highest**.

BENEDICTUS
**Blessed is he who comes
in the name of the Lord.
Hosanna in the highest.**

THANKSGIVING FOR CHRIST
Blessed are you, O God,
and blessed are your messengers and prophets

who have proclaimed good news to the poor
and liberty to captives.
Blessed is your servant Mary
and the holy child of her womb,
born to make known your mysteries,
to seek out and to save what is lost in life,
and to heal and bring wholeness
by the forgiveness of sins.
Blessed is he
who in life and in death revealed your glory,
who was betrayed and rejected,
abused and killed,
but who rose at the third day's dawn
and awakens in us the hope
that all powers of evil will fall
and the earth will be saved from its enemies.

NARRATIVE
Jesus had taught his disciples
that to find life was first to lose it
and had spoken of the sufferings that would be his.
On the night when he was betrayed,
Jesus took bread,
and having blessed it,
he broke the bread,
and gave it to his disciples, saying:
'Take, eat.
This is my body which is broken for you.
This do in remembrance of me.'
In the same way he took wine,
and having given thanks for it,
he poured it out,
and gave the cup to his disciples, saying:
'This cup is the new covenant in my blood.
This do, as often as you drink it,
in remembrance of me.'

MEMORIAL PROCLAMATION
Remembering his eternal self-giving,
we proclaim the mystery of Christ among us.
Made one with him,
and thus one with each other,
we offer these gifts
and with them ourselves,
a single, holy living sacrifice.

INVOCATION
Come upon us with your Holy Spirit, O God,
and upon this bread and this wine,
that we may be renewed once again,
and that in being healed within,
the whole of life might be made new for us.

INTERCESSIONS
In this mystery of communion with Christ,
let us remember with thanksgiving
those who have gone before us
and through whom life has flowed to us,
and with the whole company of saints
in heaven and on earth
let us be making our prayers of intercession
for the life of the world
[here free prayer may be offered]
through Christ.

DOXOLOGY
By whom,
with whom,
in whom,
in the unity of the Holy Spirit,
all glory and honour is yours, almighty God,
world without end.
Amen.

THE LORD'S PRAYER
Lord, teach us to pray together:

Our Father . . .

BREAKING OF THE BREAD
God's holy one
gives his life
for the life of the world.

AGNUS DEI
Lamb of God,
who takes away the sin of the world:
have mercy upon us.
Lamb of God,
who takes away the sin of the world:
have mercy upon us.
Lamb of God,
who takes away the sin of the world:
grant us your peace.

COMMUNION

PEACE
The peace of the Lord Jesus Christ be with you.
Let us greet one another with a sign of peace.

THE SENDING OUT

CLOSING PRAYER
Let it be according to your will, O God.
Let there be justice in the nations,
let there be forgiveness among people,
and let us learn to love our enemies.
Let the hungry be fed, O God,
let the poor receive in abundance,

and let us learn to be kind
even to those who are ungrateful.
Let those who weep laugh again,
let those who suffer hear news of deliverance,
and let us and all people
learn to be merciful as you are merciful, O God.
With you nothing is impossible.
Glory, glory in the highest,
and on earth let there be peace.

A HYMN *may be sung*

DISMISSAL AND BENEDICTION
Go now in peace.
The grace of our Lord Jesus Christ,
the love of God,
and the communion of the Holy Spirit,
be with you.
Amen.

DAY SIX
The Apostle to the Hebrews

THE PREPARATION

INTROIT Psalm

A HYMN *may be sung*

OPENING SENTENCE AND PRAYER
Christ is our merciful and faithful high priest. Tested by what
he suffered, he is able to help those who are being tested.
Hebrews 2.17, 18

Lord have mercy upon us.
Christ have mercy upon us.
Lord have mercy upon us.

Almighty God,
to whom all hearts are open,
all desires known,
and from whom no secrets are hidden:
cleanse the thoughts of our hearts
by the inspiration of your Holy Spirit,
that we may perfectly love you,
and worthily magnify your holy name;
through Christ our Lord.
Amen.

THE LITURGY OF THE WORD

SCRIPTURES

SILENCE *may be kept*

SUMMARY *of the Law may be read*
Jesus said, 'You shall love the Lord your God with all your heart, and with all your soul, and with all your mind. This is the greatest and first commandment. And the second is like it: You shall love your neighbour as yourself.' *Matthew 22*

REFLECTION/SERMON

THE LITURGY OF THE SACRAMENT

A HYMN may be sung

OFFERING
Blessed are you, O God of all creation,
through whose goodness we have this bread to offer,
which earth has given and human hands have made;
may it become for us the bread of life.

Blessed are you, O God of all creation,
through whose goodness we have this wine to offer,
fruit of the vine and work of human hands;
may it become for us the cup of blessing.

Receive these gifts, dear God,
and accept in them the sacrifice of ourselves.
In life and in death
may we be an offering to you for ever.

DIALOGUE
The Lord be with you.
And also with you.
Lift up your hearts.
We lift them to the Lord.
Let us give thanks to the Lord our God.
It is right to give him thanks and praise.

PREFACE TO THE THANKSGIVING
We offer you praise
and hearts lifted high, O God,
who in the beginning
formed the heavens and the earth,
all that is seen
being made from that which is not visible.
The worlds will perish, O God,
but you remain;
they wear out like clothing,
but your years never end.
And so with heaven's messengers of light,
and the whole company of saints who enfold us,
we join in the song of your unending greatness.

SANCTUS
Holy, holy, holy Lord,
God of power and might,
heaven and earth are full of your glory.
Hosanna in the highest.

BENEDICTUS
Blessed is he who comes
in the name of the Lord.
Hosanna in the highest.

THANKSGIVING FOR CHRIST
Blessed are you, O God,
whose angels,
like encircling winds and flames of fire,
have ministered your mystery through the ages;
whose prophets,
filled with visions of justice,
have spoken your word;
and whose Son,
the very image of your goodness,
has reflected in the things of earth

the glory of heaven.
We bless you for Christ,
who, as high priest of our salvation,
offered himself,
enduring the cross,
to free us and all people
from bondage to the fear of death.

NARRATIVE
On the night when he was betrayed,
Jesus took bread,
and having blessed it,
he broke the bread,
and gave it to his disciples, saying:
'Take, eat.
This is my body which is broken for you.
This do in remembrance of me.'
In the same way he took wine,
and having given thanks for it,
he poured it out,
and gave the cup to his disciples, saying:
'This cup is the new covenant in my blood.
This do, as often as you drink it,
in remembrance of me.'

MEMORIAL PROCLAMATION
Remembering his eternal self-giving,
we proclaim the mystery of Christ among us.
Made one with him,
and thus one with each other,
we offer these gifts
and with them ourselves,
a single, holy living sacrifice.

INVOCATION
O Christ,
who ever lives in life's inner sanctuary,

and is the same
yesterday, today and forever,
as you blessed your first disciples
with the Holy Spirit
so bless us here and this bread and wine,
that in receiving them into ourselves
we may be strengthened within,
nourished with the goodness of God.

INTERCESSIONS
In this mystery of communion with Christ,
let us remember with thanksgiving
those who have gone before us
and through whom life has flowed to us,
and with the whole company of saints
in heaven and on earth
let us be making our prayers of intercession
for the life of the world
[*here free prayer may be offered*]
through Christ.

DOXOLOGY
By whom,
with whom,
in whom,
in the unity of the Holy Spirit,
all glory and honour is yours, almighty God,
world without end.
Amen.

THE LORD'S PRAYER
Lord, teach us to pray together:

Our Father . . .

116

BREAKING OF THE BREAD
Christ offers himself
for the life of the world.

AGNUS DEI
Lamb of God,
who takes away the sin of the world:
have mercy upon us.
Lamb of God,
who takes away the sin of the world:
have mercy upon us.
Lamb of God,
who takes away the sin of the world:
grant us your peace.

COMMUNION

PEACE
The peace of the Lord Jesus Christ be with you.
Let us greet one another with a sign of peace.

THE SENDING OUT

CLOSING PRAYER
O God,
who has called us
as sisters and brothers of Christ,
and placed your laws in our minds
and written them on our hearts,
as you have been our God
so may we be your faithful people,
living together in mutual love
and inwardly growing

in the assurance of things hoped for
and the conviction of things not yet seen.
With all people may we work
to build sure foundations for life,
so that when the heavens and earth pass away
we may remain in what cannot be shaken.
Amen.

A HYMN *may be sung*

DISMISSAL AND BENEDICTION
Go now in peace.
The grace of our Lord Jesus Christ,
the love of God,
and the communion of the Holy Spirit,
be with you.
Amen.

DAY SEVEN
St John the Divine

THE PREPARATION

INTROIT Psalm

A HYMN may be sung

OPENING SENTENCE AND PRAYER
'Listen,' says Jesus. 'I am standing at the door knocking; if you
hear my voice and open the door, I will come in to you and
eat with you, and you with me.' *Revelation 3.20*

Lord have mercy upon us.
Christ have mercy upon us.
Lord have mercy upon us.

Almighty God,
to whom all hearts are open,
all desires known,
and from whom no secrets are hidden:
cleanse the thoughts of our hearts
by the inspiration of your Holy Spirit,
that we may perfectly love you,
and worthily magnify your holy name;
through Jesus Christ our Lord.
Amen.

THE LITURGY OF THE WORD

SCRIPTURES

SILENCE may be kept

SUMMARY *of the Law may be read*
Jesus said, 'You shall love the Lord your God with all your
heart, and with all your soul, and with all your mind. This is
the greatest and first commandment. And the second is like it:
You shall love your neighbour as yourself.' *Matthew 22*

REFLECTION/SERMON

THE LITURGY OF THE SACRAMENT

A HYMN *may be sung*

OFFERING
Blessed are you, O God of all creation,
through whose goodness we have this bread to offer,
which earth has given and human hands have made;
may it become for us the bread of life.

Blessed are you, O God of all creation,
through whose goodness we have this wine to offer,
fruit of the vine and work of human hands;
may it become for us the cup of blessing.

Receive these gifts, dear God,
and accept in them the sacrifice of ourselves.
In life and in death
may we be an offering to you for ever.

DIALOGUE
The Lord be with you.
And also with you.
Lift up your hearts.
We lift them to the Lord.
Let us give thanks to the Lord our God.
It is right to give him thanks and praise.

PREFACE TO THE THANKSGIVING
We offer you praise
and hearts lifted high, O God,
who is and was and is to come,
the beginning and the end,
and from whom flows
the river of the waters of life
in heaven and on earth.
We praise you,
we bless you,
we worship you,
for your holiness dwells among us
like the silence of the night,
and your Spirit awakens life
like the stirrings of a mighty wind.
And so with everything that worships
day and night in the whole temple of creation,
with the burning sun and angels of light
and with all that is conscious and vibrant with life
we join in the song of your unending greatness.

SANCTUS
Holy, holy, holy Lord,
God of power and might,
heaven and earth are full of your glory.
Hosanna in the highest.

BENEDICTUS
Blessed is he who comes
in the name of the Lord.
Hosanna in the highest.

THANKSGIVING FOR CHRIST
Blessed are you, O God,
and blessed is your son, Jesus,
born to proclaim an everlasting gospel of grace

and to overcome the world's deceiver
and evil's depths of destruction.
Blessed is he who was persecuted,
who died for our freedom
and yet is alive for ever,
who guides us to life's wellspring
that we may receive from it freely
and be strengthened to endure in hope
until all forces of wrong are thrown down
and death itself is destroyed,
when you will have made all things new, O God,
and mourning and crying and pain will be no more.

NARRATIVE
It was in speaking of the fulfilment
of the mystery of salvation
that Jesus on the night when he was betrayed
took bread,
and having blessed it,
he broke the bread,
and gave it to his disciples, saying:
'Take, eat.
This is my body which is broken for you.
This do in remembrance of me.'
In the same way he took wine,
and having given thanks for it,
he poured it out,
and gave the cup to his disciples, saying:
'This cup is the new covenant in my blood.
This do, as often as you drink it,
in remembrance of me.'

MEMORIAL PROCLAMATION
Remembering his eternal self-giving,
we proclaim the mystery of Christ among us.

Made one with him,
and thus one with each other,
we offer these gifts
and with them ourselves,
a single, holy living sacrifice.

INVOCATION
Come, O Holy Spirit of God,
and bless us and this bread and wine.
Renew in us the freshness of first love
that we may passionately hold
to the faith of Jesus,
and that, even in dying,
we may know ourselves to be free of death.

INTERCESSIONS
In this mystery of communion with Christ,
let us remember with thanksgiving
those who have gone before us
and through whom life has flowed to us,
and with the whole company of saints
in heaven and on earth
let us be making our prayers of intercession
for the life of the world
[*here free prayer may be offered*]
through Christ.

DOXOLOGY
By whom,
with whom,
in whom,
in the unity of the Holy Spirit,
all glory and honour is yours, almighty God,
world without end.
Amen.

THE LORD'S PRAYER
Lord, teach us to pray together:

Our Father . . .

BREAKING OF THE BREAD
The Lamb
slain
for the life of the world.

AGNUS DEI
Lamb of God,
who takes away the sin of the world:
have mercy upon us.
Lamb of God,
who takes away the sin of the world:
have mercy upon us.
Lamb of God,
who takes away the sin of the world:
grant us your peace.

COMMUNION

PEACE
The peace of the Lord Jesus Christ be with you.
Let us greet one another with a sign of peace.

THE SENDING OUT

CLOSING PRAYER
At the rising of the sun and at its setting
men and women throughout the world
have been celebrating your holy presence
in bread and wine, O Christ.
So may we know your presence
in the whole of life.

Come and open wide
within us and around us
the portals of heaven
that we may see your glory
as the very light of life.
Come that war and sorrow
may be banished from the world
and that we and all people
might no longer be misled.
Come for the healing of the nations,
for the healing of earth's brokenness
and our own brokenness.
Come, O Christ, come quickly,
for salvation is of you.

A HYMN *may be sung*

DISMISSAL AND BENEDICTION
Go now in peace.
The grace of our Lord Jesus Christ,
the love of God,
and the communion of the Holy Spirit,
be with you.
Amen.

Part Three

MEDITATIONS ON ST LUKE'S GOSPEL

INTRODUCTION

These three sets of meditations on the birth, death and resurrection of Jesus have been developed in the context of prayer and reflection during Advent and Christmas, Holy Week and the season of Easter. They can, of course, be used outside these specific times and seasons, for the themes of birth and death and new life are interwoven throughout the whole of the Christian year, and even beyond that into most religious thought and practice throughout the world. Even those who do not consider themselves religious will reflect upon the things of birth and death. They will wonder about those who have gone before them, and certainly will desire for themselves and their loved ones new beginnings out of endings in life. The meditations have taken these themes that touch the experience, the fears and hopes, of all people, and have attempted to reflect upon them in the light of the Christian belief in the birth, death and resurrection of the One who called himself the Son of Man. In the story of his nativity, the birth of every child is contemplated; in the account of his crucifixion, the death of every woman and man is reflected upon; and in the event of his resurrection, humanity's hope for new life is expressed.

Like the other prayers in this book these meditations can be used in a variety of worship contexts and settings for prayer together, as well as simply being used for silent individual contemplation. If they are used publicly, it is important not to rush through them. Frequent pauses, not just where it says 'silence', will allow the images to settle more deeply, enabling a more sustained contemplation of the themes. As well as deciding in advance not to be rushed in leading the meditations, it is important to create an atmosphere that is still. To do without electric lighting, for instance, or to subdue the lighting and make use of candlelight are practical ways of encouraging greater interior attentiveness. And because the meditations draw on our common experiences of birth and death and hopes for new life, it is best to read the words not so much *to* the people as *from among* the people. A praying from the midst will evoke among a congregation a greater sense of identity with the prayers, and will allow the words to become their words, their expressions of joy and pain and hope, for themselves and for the world.

THE SEVEN STAGES OF BIRTH

THE FIRST
And the angel said to Zechariah, 'Do not be afraid, for your prayer has been heard.' *Luke 1.13*

Let us pray:

Holy, holy, holy,
Lord God of hosts,
the whole earth is full of your glory,
and we bless you.
With those before us over the centuries
and with women and men throughout the world today
in sanctuaries of prayer
and holy places everywhere,
we offer up our sacrifice of praise,
an offering that joins
what is like a great cloud of incense
rising from every age and every nation.
Not just in houses of prayer
and corners of reflection;
not just in the hours of religious observance,
or in the inner place and quiet of our souls,
but in the whole temple of creation,
from the rising of the sun to its setting,
from the beginning of time to its end.
With everything that has been called into being,
with the light of the stars of the heavens,
and with all that breathes and has motion,
we cry: 'Glory'.
We give thanks, O God,
that here in this temple of prayer
many before us have glimpsed your presence

within them and around them
and have been assured
that at the heart of life's glory
glows your love for each one and each created thing.
And so whether our spirits are confident or unsure,
and whether we struggle
amidst death and barrenness
or are uplifted by the exhilarations of life
and new conception,
we take time now to ponder and to give thanks
that your message of love is now,
as it has always been,
'Do not be afraid'.

Silence

The fears that are in us
which have not yet been cast out by love,
and the forces that paralyse and frighten the world
which have not yet been dispersed,
we offer now in prayer:
for nations and whole societies
held hostage by hatred and conflict,
for communities and neighbourhoods
embittered by division and prejudice,
for relationships and family life
inhibited by hurts suffered
sometimes from one generation to the next,
and for individuals who fear the future
because they have not been strengthened by the past.
And what we pray for all people, O God,
we ask also for ourselves:
that we may know your Spirit
residing within our spirits,
stronger than the temptations that overwhelm us
or the darknesses that settle upon us,
more confident than the uncertainties that worry us

or the losses that shake us,
and more creative than any barrenness or ending
that leaves us without hope.
And as we offer these yearnings
from our lives and for the world,
may we know
with an assurance beyond our comprehending
that these prayers
and the prayers of all hearts
are heard by you, O God,
in love.

THE SECOND
And the angel said to Mary: 'The Holy Spirit will come upon
you, and the power of the Most High will overshadow you;
therefore the child to be born of you will be holy.' *Luke 1.35*

Let us pray:

Blessed are you, O God,
whose Spirit in the beginning
brooded over the face of the waters
to bring forth creation in all its splendour,
and whose power of life through the ages
has overshadowed matter
to call forth vitality and consciousness from the ground.
We bless you
for the welling up of life that you have summoned
and which surges from depths beneath our seeing;
for plant forms and fruits
which emerge from the dark soil
with an abundance of colour and scent,
of taste and goodness;
for life forms that appear within the seas
and from the depths of ocean darkness,
strange in texture and movement and seeing;

and for planets and lights of the sky
that appear beyond numbering
out of the infinite stretches of space.
We give thanks for the life,
both physical and spiritual,
seen and unseen,
that issues from within us,
the seeds of new beginnings and births,
the conceptions of imagination and new generation.
The goodness born of these depths, O God,
is holy,
for you are holy
and all life is of you.

Silence

That out of the great voids of space and time,
and out of the barrenness
that can be within and between people,
you have at moments, O God,
brought forth not only life
but an abundance
which we could not have imagined,
these things lead us
to be offering our prayers in hope,
for there is no emptiness
out of which life is impossible with you.
And so for our friends and loved ones
and for the world we pray.
Where there is despair of healing between people
who are torn by violence and by bitterness of memory;
where there is a ceasing to believe
that wrongs done to the earth and to one another
can somehow be redeemed;
and where there is a giving up hope
that we have the resources
to begin again out of failure and shame,

grant us, O God,
new ways of seeing
and hoping
and believing together.
Like a wind that carries in its currents
the seeds of new life,
so move among us
and through us,
implanting the hopes of fresh beginnings
that what before seemed impossible
in our lives and in the world
might become instead
ground that is prepared and open to the Spirit.

THE THIRD
Then Mary said to the angel, 'Here am I, the servant of the
Lord; let it be with me according to your word.' *Luke 1.38*

Let us pray:

O God of life,
of all life,
of each life,
who in love has called forth the whole of creation
in its many forms and shapes and stages,
we bless you for your presence of light
that is among us and within,
the light that has sustained all life before us
and which enlightens every soul coming into the world.
We give thanks for the gift of your favour
that rests on each created thing,
each mother and child,
each life form and species,
and without which nothing that is would be.
Having been chosen for life,
with bodies that share earth's vitality,

with minds alive with consciousness,
and with spirits reflective of the everlasting image,
we give thanks in the great mystery,
and offer ourselves as servants
of the life that is in all things.
Let it be with us according to your will, O God,
let us be so sure of the eternal
that we can be at peace in the movement of time,
and let us so see you in the things of time
that we may know ourselves to be part of the eternal.
And as you have loved and cherished us
so may we love and cherish one another,
and in learning to love ourselves
come to love you in all life.

Silence

Let us now pray for those
who do not know themselves to be favoured,
and in not knowing love
have neither loved themselves
nor others as themselves:
for children
who grow up with no certainty that they are precious,
whose innocence and original beauty
are being marred by neglect and abuse,
and who experience
neither the safety of physical protection
nor the assurance of being held in affection;
for individuals
who because of appearance or class or gender
are denied acceptance and opportunity,
and who come to doubt
their own worth
and their own ability;
for whole communities and societies,
who year after year,

or even generation after generation,
are made to feel small and insignificant
and whose lives and relationships and culture
no longer bear the marks of confidence and self-dignity;
and for ourselves and all people,
that even in the midst of loss
or rejection
or betrayal,
we may know ourselves to be favoured by you, O God,
and that whether we live
or whether we die,
we are,
each one,
chosen
to be bearers of the everlasting.

THE FOURTH
And Mary remained with Elizabeth about three months and
then returned to her home. *Luke 1.56*

Let us pray:

We worship you,
we bless you,
we magnify you, O God.
Our souls are glad
and we rejoice in your gift of life to us.
And we know,
not only within ourselves
but through one another,
in the great interweaving of our spirits and lives,
that you have done marvellous and unexpected things.
We give thanks that amidst wrongs
and domination and oppression,
which we witness from afar
or which touch us directly,

we see also signs of hope
and new beginnings and deliverance,
and that some of these signs
we see not only without
but feel within
like the leaping of life in our depths.
And so we bless you
that over the centuries before us
and throughout the world today,
as in the history of our own souls,
although destructive powers have held sway
and proud forces have suppressed
what is good and simple,
we have seen also
that the end of evildoing is death
and that the most mighty strongholds of power
can topple in a day and in a night.
We give thanks
for the liberations from wrong that have occurred
and which point
to the final freedom from death's powers
and the promised day of justice.
For these outward signs of salvation,
and for the times also when our inner emptiness
has been satisfied by you,
we give thanks, O God,
and in remembering and giving thanks
we are renewed again in hope.

Silence

Let us pray for those who wait with hope:
for those who hope
because they have felt within themselves
the stirrings of new life,
and so believe expectantly;

for those who hope
because they have been promised new possibilities,
and so watch with eagerness;
and for those who hope against hope
and having reached dark depths in their lives
choose not to despair
but still yearn for release.
And so we offer our prayers
for all sorts of people
in all sorts of conditions:
for women and men who wait in excitement
for the birth of a child
or for new beginnings in relationships,
and whose hopes are mixed with fear and apprehension;
for those who wait for messages
that will bring them news of loved ones
and who in silence are left wondering;
and for individuals and whole societies
who search for signs of new openings
in work and health and peace,
and who sometimes feel
that their waiting has been in vain
and that final opportunities have passed them by.
Like those who watch for the morning, O God,
so we and all those who hope for new light
wait expectantly,
longing for the goodness you have promised.
As we wait and watch for what you will do
in the lives of those whom we love
and in the not yet discovered realms of our own lives,
may we know with an inner assurance
that as well as the moments of birth
you have given us also the waiting times, O God.
Strengthen us in the way of patient endurance,
the endurance that produces hope and salvation.

THE FIFTH
And the time came for Mary to deliver her child; and she gave
birth to a son. *Luke 2.6–7*

Let us pray:

Glory, glory, glory,
for your child born among us, O God,
a promised birth,
conceived and awaited in love,
delivered and born in labour,
heaven's son come among us,
sent to redeem the earth.
Glory, glory, glory.
The stars of the open sky
and lights of distant galaxies,
the brightness of the morning sun
and the moon's whiteness at night,
all glow with gladness at this birth.
The glistening across the waters
and light dazzling off snow,
the brilliance of mountain peaks
and the whole earth's radiance,
shine forth a welcome to the Saviour.
And with them we join our voices across the ages
and say, 'Glory, glory, glory
to God ever born among us,
to the Light still coming into the world,
to the Christ sent to save every age
and all creation from sin.'
We give thanks for everything that is of you, O God,
and that is born from within us:
for our children formed from your substance
and given birth through our flesh;
for the gifts of creativity and imagination
flowing for ever from you
and finding expression

140

in the utterance and actions of time;
and for the love that first conceived of life
and then of new beginnings,
which startles us out of wrongdoing
with forgiveness,
and inspires our souls
with hopes for peace.
That in all of this
you are born among us
in spirit and in matter,
in ways seen and unseen,
these things lead us to say,
'Glory to you, O God, for the Christ born this day'.

Silence

Let us pray
for those who do not know God with them
and who cannot believe
that God's life is born from within:
for men and women
whose inner selves are tormented or empty
and whose souls do not seem like the womb
from which salvation is born;
and for those whose family lives and relationships
or societies and nations
are so overwhelmed by conflict
that the light of life is hidden from sight.
Let us pray for those
who are in the midst of struggle and labour,
and whose journeys are hard:
for individuals and whole communities
whose painful times
might yet be birth pangs of new beginnings;
and for the many who are weighed down by uncertainties
and yearn to be freed of their burdens.
And we pray too

for those who know fresh stirrings of life
but are unsure about the way ahead
and have not yet found people and places
of welcome and acceptance
for the new thing that is happening within them.
And what we pray for all people, O God,
we ask also for ourselves,
that we may know and cherish
the life of your Spirit planted within us,
and be strengthened
in the labouring
and the loving
of our lives.

THE SIXTH
And Mary treasured all these things and pondered them in
her heart. *Luke 2.19*

Let us pray:

In the stillness of this place
and aware of the quiet prayers
and silent ponderings of many before us here,
whose prayers like gentle murmurings of the past
still ripple within these walls,
we too take time, O God,
to pause and to wonder.
With men and women of every nation
we treasure in our hearts the memory,
the holy story
of messengers of promise,
stirrings of new life,
excitement and anticipation,
all leading to the nativity of our salvation,
Christ born on earth,
light of your light,

glory of your glory,
born to save all creation and every person
from the darkness and confusions of sin.
And so we gather
to ponder the mystery of your life among us,
and in pondering
to be renewed again in hope
and in gratitude of spirit.
For the most treasured gifts of life
within and around us, O God,
we give thanks:
for your sacred image
planted deep and ineradicably in the earth,
and for your beauty and goodness
hidden within men and women
and revealed in creativity and faithfulness together
and in the giving and receiving of love and generosity.
We give thanks for treasured memories,
for the birth of our children,
for the discovery of affections,
for enduring friendship,
and for the fond recollections
of those who have gone before us.
For everything that is born of your Spirit on earth,
and especially the peace that is within and between people,
and the goodwill that issues from individual hearts
and extends to all creation,
we give glory to you, O God.

Silence

Let us pray for peace on earth and goodwill among people:
for peace in places of conflict,
in nations torn by the violence of war,
in societies fractured by hatred and misunderstandings,
in families embittered by past wrongs;
and where there is indifference and hostility

let us pray for the coming of goodwill,
in people who have lost respect for one another,
in those whose vision is narrowed by selfish desire
or whose relationships are undermined by suspicion.
And as we pray for the great things
of peace and goodwill among the nations,
let us with confidence pray also for ourselves,
in the certainty that peace in our own hearts
and goodwill among us in our daily relationships
are part of the coming of peace for all people.
Let us pray
for those whom we most cherish,
for our friends and family.
We commend them to your providential care, O God,
as we commend all people,
in the belief that they are,
each one,
treasured in love by you.

THE SEVENTH
And Mary and Joseph brought the child to Jerusalem to present him to the Lord. *Luke 2.22*

Let us pray:

Blessed are you, O God of all creation,
from whom,
through whom,
and to whom are all things.
From you we have come in the great mystery
and to you we return.
From you we have received grace upon grace,
a tenderness of mercy and forgiveness
within our ever-living souls,
and all around us in creation
glory upon glory,

heaven's abundance of beauty on earth.
To you we present ourselves
and all that has been born of your Spirit in us.
As well as the complexity of our lives
we offer our simplicity and childlikeness.
As well as our life experience and strength
we offer our innocence and vulnerability.
Assure us again, O God,
of your loving acceptance,
so that more and more
we may know the life in us
and in all people
to be blessed by you for ever.
We give thanks, O God,
for the things of your salvation
that our eyes have seen,
in the quiet events of daily life and relationships
and in public places for all to see:
for willingness to forgive and begin again,
for courage to speak and act against wrong,
and for the desire in people to love and be loved.
We give thanks
for the light of your glory among us,
Christ born on earth,
the light that shines in creation's flesh and matter,
given for all people
and for the whole world's salvation.

Silence

Let us pray
that the gift of life may be redeemed,
that we and all people may find again
the goodness that lies at the heart of creation
and be liberators of it in all things.
For places in our world
where whole populations and races

are regarded with hatred and inhumanity,
and for individuals in our societies and neighbourhoods
who are viewed as irredeemable
because of illnesses or mistakes or peculiarities.
And what we ask for individuals and communities
let us pray also for nations
and even for the whole earth,
that we may seek a redeeming
of what is good and true and beautiful
in our shared life and cultures,
and be alert and receptive to the glory
that lies hidden in creation's elements around us.
And as we look for the redemption of what is good
and pray for those who promote wholeness and healing,
let us pray also for ourselves,
that more and more we may grow in the conviction
that there is no part of us,
no failure of our past,
no weakness of our present
that cannot be transformed by love.
Strengthen us in such a hope, O God,
that in good and bad times alike,
and when sadness and suffering pierce our souls,
we may know that nothing on earth
and nothing above or beneath us
is beyond the power of your redemption.

THE SEVEN STAGES OF DEATH

THE FIRST
The chief priests and the scribes were looking for a way to put
him to death. *Luke 22.2*

Let us pray:

In this place over the years
people have gathered
to ponder the great mysteries of God
and to find more light
for their lives and for their world.
Like them we come
looking to the One who is above and beyond us
and at the very heart of life.
Like them we come
in the hope of finding forgiveness
and new strength for living
from the wellsprings of God's grace
deep in this place,
inexhaustible.
Let us give thanks for places such as this,
for times of silence and reflection and inner renewal,
for those before us and now
who are like guardians of the holy,
opening the glory of the invisible to us,
and who are guides in wisdom
pointing to the way we are to live.
Let us give thanks for these ones,
but not naïvely.
Let us give thanks,
while not forgetting
that it was priests of the holy place

and moral leaders of the holy city
who looked for ways to get rid of Jesus.
And so as we give thanks
for the great and rich religious tradition
to which we belong,
let us also ask ourselves
what it is we feel threatened by,
what it is we try to reject –
for the Holy One of God,
who is much greater than the bounded Scriptures
and sacraments and cherished places of our religion,
is present among us,
still challenging,
often unsettling,
always inviting us
to grow more and more into the everlasting image,
summoning us,
if we will hear,
to a love that is beyond ever being comfortably bounded,
whether by the ancient walls of our tradition
or the commonly agreed boundaries
of how much we are to love
and who we are to love.

Silence

Let us pray for our church,
for our churches,
for religious and moral leaders
of every place and every tradition,
that there might be greater clarity of vision
to see the glory of heaven in earth
and to see also the forces of darkness among us
that threaten to belittle or destroy what is good,
and for an openness to being ever expanded
in the ways of generosity
and in the practice of forgiveness.
And not only for our leaders

but for ourselves and all people let us pray,
that we may have the confidence to open ourselves
to the ever-new demands of going out in love to others,
while also knowing how to protect the boundaries
that make for well-being and security
in ourselves and all who need protecting.
May our eyes be opened,
may our imaginations be enlivened
so that we may see
and encourage others to see
the holiness that indwells all life.
Let us pray for those
who have little
religious and moral inheritance to draw on,
for those
who have not been given keys of language and tradition
that will unlock for them
~~gates of the eternal in the midst of time,~~ *the mystery of God's love*
or who have received insufficient love in their lives
to enable them to live with dignity
and with a largeness of spirit towards others.
And what we pray for all people
let us ask also for ourselves,
that we may treasure the truth and the wisdom
which we have received,
and be alert and humble enough
to receive enlargements of that truth
from unexpected directions.
Come, come, Lord Jesus,
and stand in our midst
as you did stand in the midst of the temple.
Open our eyes to your unbounded love
for we too would be free,
not from the goodness of our traditions,
but free within them
to see you and to love you
in all that is.

THE SECOND
He knelt down and prayed: 'Father, if you are willing, remove
this cup from me.' *Luke 22.42*

Let us pray:

As we reflect on the events of the passion
and hold in our minds too
the sufferings that continue today
in the lives of men and women and children
throughout the world,
in situations of war and ethnic cleansing,
in loss and separation and bereavement,
in struggles against disease
and inner torments of mind and soul,
let us set all these things
in the context of the goodness that is longed for.
What was it that Jesus desired to be delivered to
when he prayed, 'Take this cup from me'?
And what is our desire
for ourselves and our loved ones
and for all who are in agony now?
Is it a desire for health and physical wholeness
that is free from pain and want?
Is it a desire for inner certainty and peace
that releases us from confusions and destructive thoughts?
Or is it a longing for outward peace
and a just ordering of our collective life
that allows for equal freedoms and opportunities,
or is it simply the desire
to know that we will wake in the morning
to the glory of the day's light,
that we will hear again the spring song of birds,
and enjoy the company and affection of friends
and taste together wholesome food
and feel the fresh wind on our faces,
and that at the end of our day and work we will rest

and expect in sleep to be refreshed
in soul and in body?
Are these the things we desire?
Do we not with all people desire them
because we have already known them in part,
as Jesus too knew them
and desired not to be deprived of them?
And so as we reflect on the passion of Jesus
and of the suffering ones in the world today,
let us view these things alongside the gift of life
that has been given and received and delighted in.
Let us give thanks for the life that is within us,
that has come down to us from the past,
for the life of thought and imagination
that wells up from our inner depths,
and for the abundance of life that surrounds us
in earth and sea and sky.

Silence

But which one of us
has received only good in life?
Which one of us has not
at different times and in different ways
joined our voice to the many before us
who in the midst of loss or fear or confusion
have prayed, 'Take this cup from me'?
If this is not our prayer now,
let us not forget the times when we have so prayed,
or when we will so pray,
and in our intercessions here let us stand
with those everywhere today
who utter prayers for deliverance:
for whole populations
who long to be freed from the violence of war;
for mothers and fathers
who witness the distress and hunger of their children;

for individuals whose inner darkness is so great
that they lose hold of life;
and for the people who see ahead of them
only agonizing moments and decisions.
O God,
the Father of our Lord Jesus Christ,
to whom each person in heaven and on earth
is brother or sister,
it is for the whole human family that we pray,
asking for release from suffering,
deliverance in our lives and in all life.
And in the mystery of our journey of return to you
may we more and more learn
to pray as Jesus did.
Not our will but yours, O God.

THE THIRD
And Jesus said, 'Judas, is it with a kiss that you are betraying
the Son of Man?' *Luke 22.48*

Let us pray:

O God,
whose love has been from the beginning
and knows no end,
who each day in the morning light
kisses the earth with life,
and in the evening
bathes it in the soft light
of the moon's whiteness,
let your face so shine upon us
in the things of heaven and earth
that we may be saved.
We give thanks for the intimations of your glory
that come to us in all these things,
in the warmth of the spring earth,

in the hearty company of a friend,
in the glowing intimacies of love.
And yet it is with a kiss that you are betrayed, O God,
a sign of heaven used for hell.
In every betrayal of earth
love again is forsaken,
and the Son of Man suffers,
a stranger, hungry,
sick, imprisoned.
We know, O God,
betrayals of which we have been a part,
of women and men,
of whole groups and peoples,
sometimes intentional,
at other times unconsciously chosen
simply as part of the interconnectedness of life.
And we know too
whether we have sought forgiveness,
whether we have attempted change.
Turn to us again, O God,
in those whom we have wronged
that we may be restored to you again.

Silence

Let us pray for those who know betrayal,
for whole populations
abandoned by nations,
for powerless people
turned against by their own governments,
for men and women
betrayed by broken promises,
for children abused
by those to whose care they have been entrusted.
Let us pray for individuals
who have been abandoned by the ones closest to them,
and have not been able to find again

peace within themselves
or new beginnings in their lives.
And as we pray for these ones,
let us pray also
for those who know the misery
of having betrayed another
and repentant have not yet found the way forward.
May we and all people know, O God,
that there is nothing that can separate us
from your love
or from the depth of your healing,
no wrong done,
no injury suffered.
Though all else may fail us
may we grow in the assurance
that at the very heart of life,
where you reside,
we will never be betrayed, O God.

THE FOURTH
But the people kept shouting, 'Crucify, crucify him!'
Luke 23.21

Let us pray:

O God,
who in the beginning
created us from spirit and matter,
children of the earth
and born from your eternal substance,
we give thanks for the light,
your light which no darkness can put out,
that enlightens every person coming into the world.
We give thanks
for the implanted wisdom in us to know what is right
and the will to do it,
for the ability to create

and the imagination and strength
to give birth to what has never been before,
for the desire to begin afresh
and the capacity to forgive
and to release one another to the freedom of life.
And yet we know also within us
dark streaks that bind us to the things of death,
inner confusions and temptations to wrong,
passions for destructiveness and domination,
and hardnesses that neither forgive nor forget.
Like the crowd, O God, we know in ourselves
the capacity to cry
'Hosanna'
and
'Crucify'.
It is this complexity of soul
that we bring with us in prayer,
and find ourselves standing
with all sorts of people
in all sorts of conditions,
innocence and guilt co-mingled.
Free us, O Holy Spirit,
from blind mobs and ugly frenzies
and from the destructive parts of us
that crowd out what is good,
so that more and more we may grow
in the image in which we have been created,
and learn to say 'Blessed' to the One who comes
with wholeness for the world.

Silence

Let us pray
for those against whom crowds have wrongfully turned,
often in the name of order and the majority's right
but neglecting the hurt that is done
to the small group,

to the disapproved of minority,
to the unpopular voice of poverty and injustice
that speaks a disturbing truth.
Let us pray
for a greater discernment among the nations
and in our own societies and circles of life,
that the just paths along which we are to move
and the wrongs against which we are to work
may be more clearly seen and pursued together
with strength and humility and generosity.
Let us pray for those
who prophetically announce life in the face of death,
who promote new possibilities of peace
when it seems there are none,
who call for the protection of the earth
when it would be easier to keep living as we do,
who demand justice for the neglected
when it would be more convenient not to have to change.
And as we commend these ones
to the further encouragement of your Spirit,
we pray also for ourselves,
that we too may hear the commandment of love
and pursue it in our lives with a confidence
that is unbound by the fear and opposition of others,
committing ourselves and all that is ours
to your judgement and your safekeeping, O God.
And in all things assure us again,
even when the stream of wrong flows most powerfully,
that the good that is in us and in all people
may be found again,
redeemed from hopelessness,
for we are each one
made in your image.

THE FIFTH
When they came to the place that is called the Skull, they cru-
cified him there with the criminals. *Luke 23.33*

Let us pray:

What have we done?
Who can believe
the wrong committed,
the sorrow suffered,
the punishment inflicted
on your Innocent One, O God,
in whom the eternal glory and goodness
shone clear and true?
What have we done?
Who can believe
the bruises and the battering,
the shame and disgrace today
imposed on guiltless men and women
throughout the world
who have done nothing to deserve
their rejections and sufferings?
Is their goodness so hidden?
Are human eyes so blind?
Standing by the scene of ugly wounds
and the nailing to a tree, and blood,
where would we have looked
to behold the form of your majesty, O God?
Would it have been to the death heap of criminals,
despised?
And where now shall we look?
To broken poured-out lives,
torn humanity
held of no account?
Is it so different now?
Is the smelly cell of a prison
or any place regarded as rejection

now no longer housing the tenderness
of your life among us?
And the things within us
and in those beside us
which are seen as so uncomely
that we don't like to look at them,
are these just to be cut off,
abandoned?
Rather, O God,
on this day which we call good
may we hope
that in the very rejected and afflicted things
of our lives and of others' lives
we may still find you
and be made whole.

Silence

Let us look at the rejected
in ourselves and in all people,
and let us look with new eyes as we pray:
for innocent life
that somehow has come to bear
the marks of the sin of the world;
for those unjustly judged
in our prisons and societies,
in our families and relationships,
who instead of being despised
can be the people and places
of your redeeming of us, O God.
And as we offer in prayer
the afflicted side of life
through which we may be made whole again,
may we learn hope as we wait and pray,
for even at the foot of the cross and dereliction
we hear the promise
of new gardens of life prepared

even for a criminal who dies.
O Jesus,
remember us
when you come into your kingdom.

THE SIXTH
Then Jesus said, 'Father, forgive them: for they do not know what they are doing.' *Luke 23.34*

Let us pray:

Can Jesus have been asking you, O God,
to forgive
even before they knew their wrongdoing?
Ought not perpetrators of wrong against innocent ones
first be forced to see?
Must they not first humble themselves for such crime
and penitently seek mercy?
Who is it that so readily forgives,
but maybe young children
and sometimes animals in their unreflecting loyalty?
But you,
whose wisdom reaches from one end of the earth to the other,
who shaped the heights and the depths of creation,
is your forgiveness that of these little ones
so freshly come from you,
that of these simple creatures
so untrained in the ways of resentment?
Is your forgiveness granted,
not from the powerful position
of being seen to be in the right,
but from the place of vulnerability
in which the wrong being done is not yet finished?
As the heavens are high above the earth
so are your ways higher than our ways, O God,
and your thoughts than our thoughts.

You are forever forgiving
and we bless you,
for we need not persuade you into forgiveness.
You are forever free
and we bless you,
for we cannot limit the measure of your grace.
Your mercy, O God,
is at the heart of life,
and of its continuing;
it is in the daily rising of the sun
and in the new life that springs from the earth.
For if you were to hold our sins against us
who could stand?
But with you there is forgiveness,
new mornings given again and again,
new life emerging
from your grace deep within creation.

Silence

And is this the forgiveness
that we also are called to?
As it is in heaven so on earth?
Let us pray for all people and for ourselves,
for the strength to forgive as we are daily forgiven,
to be people of grace,
free and strong in our spirit when wrong is done to us,
as wrong will be done.
But may our strength of forgiving
not weaken our naming of wrong,
and may our fighting of wrong
not feed the shadows and ill will in us too.
For nations and for people who have been wronged
and for ourselves in our own hurts,
may we know the flow of forgiveness that leads to life
and be freed from the hardness of heart
that leads to bitterness and death.

And sometimes, O God,
even more than the strength to forgive,
we need the strength to open ourselves to being forgiven,
to acknowledge the wrong in and among us
as nations and races,
as societies and religions,
as men and women in relationships.
Free us
from not knowing the wrongs that we do to one another,
and in knowing them to confess them,
and in confessing to find new life.
And may we so believe in your forgiveness
that we place our confidence in your love alone
and not in the false security of claiming to be right.
For if you so set us free, O God,
we will be free indeed.

THE SEVENTH

Then Jesus, crying with a loud voice, said, 'Father, into your
hands I commend my spirit.' And having said this, he
breathed his last. *Luke 23.46*

Let us pray:

Betrayed by a follower,
denied by a friend,
deserted and abandoned;
denounced by the religious,
rejected by crowds,
and condemned by the state;
forsaken and alone on the cross,
it was into your hands, O God,
that your servant commended his spirit.
In the midst of his weakness
he turned to your strength,
the life within all life.

As he had come into the world with nothing,
so now he parted.
Blessed are you, O God,
for you give life
and receive it again to yourself.
As angels had hovered like midwives at his birth,
so now the outstretched arms of heaven's company
waited to receive him through death's contractions.
You are the Alpha and the Omega,
the beginning and the end.

Silence

Remembering Christ's crucifixion,
we cannot but think also of nations and people,
of men and women and children
in the midst of betrayal,
dispensed with,
rejected.
And standing with all who are forsaken,
in weakness we commend them and ourselves to you, O God.
You are the true vine
without whom we can do nothing.
All things will pass but you remain.
May we know now
and in the time of our own trials
the greatest strength,
the choosing to commend ourselves into your care, O God,
for in you is the fountain of life.
But Jesus' last words were spoken
as the prayer of his whole life.
It was his strength and his weakness,
his love and his fears;
it was his life as well as his moment of death
that he commended to you, O God.
These words consummate his life,
for he died as he had lived,

and as he had taught others to live.
'Consider the lilies of the field,
and are you not of more value even than these?'
It was not because he was careless
of what was to come that he was able to say,
'Take no thought for the morrow',
but because he knew in whom he had his being.
And so
it is not just the rejected
of our world and lives
that we commend in prayer, O God,
but the whole of life,
our strengths and gifts,
the greatness of our inheritance,
the richness of our culture,
the creativity of our imagination,
the health and loveliness of our families,
as well as our need and weakness.
All that is ours and all that we are part of
we commend into your hands, O God,
our life, all life, each life,
our world,
for from you it came and to you it returns.

THE SEVEN STAGES OF RESURRECTION

THE FIRST
On the first day of the week, at early dawn, they found the
stone rolled away from the tomb. *Luke 24.1–2*

Let us pray:

Alleluia, alleluia, alleluia!
The stone of death has been rolled away.
Alleluia!
Christ is risen from the dead,
the first-born of the new creation.
Alleluia!
The powers of hell
have lost their terrifying sway,
and even in death we are free from the grave.
Alleluia, alleluia, alleluia!
We give thanks, O God,
that the tomb
in which the loveliest of men was laid
is empty,
unable to bind life to decay,
powerless to shroud the glory and the beauty
of Jesus and his love.
Alleluia!
We give thanks
that the women who held him most dear
received into their hearts
the words of the messengers of light
that he is alive.
Alleluia!
And we give thanks
that the same belief

is deep in the souls of men and women
through the centuries,
and is found at the very heart of our own faith
for we have known in our lives
your gift of life
where it seemed there was only death,
and within ourselves
we cherish the most precious hope
that those who have gone before us
still live in you and you in them,
intimations of the final day
when death itself will be rolled away
to reveal that in our living
and in our dying
you are the resurrection and the life.
Alleluia, alleluia, alleluia!

Silence

In the midst of celebrating Christ risen,
and in giving thanks for the resurrection life
that is within us and all around us,
we pray also
for the things in our lives
and in the lives of people everywhere
that are trapped in the tombs of death:
for despair in the midst of loss or confusion,
for bitterness as a result of hurt or disloyalty,
for violence of heart and of hand
in the face of conflict and opposition.
Wherever death is found,
whether in our minds and souls,
or in the matter and relationships
of our bodies and corporate lives,
lead us, O God,
by your messengers of light
to look for new life,

not among the dead
but through the pangs of death and beyond it
to the One who is alive for ever.

THE SECOND
But their eyes were kept from recognising him. *Luke 24.16*

Let us pray:

O Christ, who died and rose again
not to depart from those who loved you
but to be ever with them,
alleluia!
O Christ, who died and rose again
not to be cut off from the rest of creation
but to live for ever in life's inner sanctuary,
alleluia, alleluia!
O Christ, who died and rose again
not to be different from us
but to be the first-fruit
of what is prepared in love for all people,
alleluia, alleluia, alleluia!
O Christ,
hidden within the eyes and bodies and souls
of everyone we meet,
in every woman and every man and every child,
hidden within the goodness of each living thing,
how often our eyes do not recognize you,
but you are there
in the most unexpected places and people of our journey,
and showing yourself always to have been there
in our families and histories and traditions.
Forgive us, O Christ,
our slowness of heart in believing.

Silence

We pray now
for those who in their life journeys
are not viewed
with eyes of recognition or affection,
who are not treated
with respect or tenderness,
and who are not listened to
with attention or delight:
for children neglected,
for men and women lonely,
for people and races dismissed,
for refugees overlooked.
And what we pray for people everywhere, O God,
we ask also for ourselves
and our families and friends,
that we may be held in love
by people who know and delight in us,
and, even more,
that when we are not so enfolded
or are ignored as insignificant or mistreated,
we may know you as ever close, O Christ,
cherishing us in love.
Open our eyes
that we may see you afresh.

THE THIRD
He took bread, blessed and broke it, and gave it to them.
Then their eyes were opened, and they recognised him.
Luke 24.30–1

Let us pray:

Have our eyes been opened, O God?
How much have we recognized you among us
in one another,
deep in our own souls,

and at the heart of all that has life:
the light within the sun's brightness,
the breath within every living creature,
the goodness within human company
and the wholeness in earth's gifts
of food and wine shared?
Have we glimpsed your presence in these things,
and merely glimpsing with inner eyes
not been able to hold you fixed in sight
before our vision fades,
yet glimpsing
have our hearts not burned within us
and assured us deep down of your presence
like those whose eyes were opened at table?
And maybe even more than
catching the merest glimmering of you in creation
or momentarily feeling your freshness in the wind
or tasting it in the fruit of the earth,
is it not when the beauty of the outward
begins to break apart
that we have glimpsed you most certainly,
like those whose eyes were opened
at the breaking of the bread
and who recognized among them
the One who died yet lives?
Has it not been in seeing life's instability
that sometimes we have been given sight
of your eternity in our midst?
Has it not been at life's edges
in our falling and failing
that you have shown yourself
to be the centre of our lives,
unshakeable?
For these glimpses of your glory,
even though they vanish,
we give thanks, O God.

Silence

We pray for those in the midst of confusion or loss,
who bewildered
in the breaking apart of life
look for what can be held on to:
for those whose countries are torn by violence,
for people displaced by war and hatred,
for families dispersed by hunger and want,
for relationships shaken by failures,
and for those who are dying
and experience a breaking apart of their very bodies.
It is for these ones
and for all people,
and it is for ourselves that we pray
when we ask
that in the midst of painful disintegrations
and brokenness in life
our eyes may be opened
to recognize you among us, O God,
and to know with a burning inner certainty
that even death opens to new life.

THE FOURTH
Jesus stood among them and said, 'Peace be with you.'
Luke 24.36

Let us pray:

Blessed are you, O God,
for the stillness that is at the heart of creation
and from which all that is comes forth.
Blessed are you
for the silence deep in life,
something of which we glimpse

in the calm of an early morning
and in an evening's stillness,
the deep peace of the quiet earth
even amidst wild winds
and swelling seas.
We give thanks for the peace
which streams from your life, O God,
and glimmers through creation,
which undergirds us
and sustains our ever-living souls,
the peace that shone most clear
in your Son risen from death,
whose words of peace
repeated through the centuries
have brought assurance
and inner certainty
and stillness of soul
to many before us in the midst of trouble.
We give thanks
that the promise of peace is uttered
not by One who evaded struggle and temptation
and pain and rejection,
but by One who suffered and died,
and whose words of peace
spoken from the other side of death
carry with them the strength of the life
that is stronger than the grave.
For this peace
which is beyond our understanding
but which sustains life
like everlasting arms beneath us,
and which has upheld
men and women of faith over the centuries
with a quiet confidence of spirit
in the midst of outward uncertainty and suffering,
we give you thanks, O God,
and for the great saints and martyrs

who having lost life have found it
and now live forever in peace.

Silence

We pray for people everywhere
who yearn today for peace,
peace for their families and nations,
for forgiveness and reconciliation in relationships,
for a release in mind and soul
from inner agonies and obsessions.
And in asking for peace and security for others,
and for safeguarding and well-being
for our loved ones and ourselves,
we ask above all else, O God,
for the peace of the risen Christ.
And so we ask
not to escape from all difficulty
but that in the midst of it,
in the struggles and uncertainties
that will inevitably be ours,
and eventually in the approach of death,
may we be rooted securely within
and know in our spirits
the peace that is at the heart of life
and grow more and more in the inner assurance
that Christ ever stands before us
on our journeys
and speaks to us words of peace.

THE FIFTH
And he said to them, 'Why are you frightened, and why do
doubts arise in your hearts?' *Luke 24.38*

Let us pray:

O God,
who is everywhere present,
in the dappling light of the morning
and in the darkness of the night,
in the full brimmed confidence of the heart
and in its times of emptiness and dejection,
what is it that frightens us
when we become aware of your presence
close to us
like the first disciples,
enough even to feel
with inner hands and eyes and heart
that we are touched and can touch you?
When we joy at your presence
knowing you with us
yet still wondering and disbelieving,
do we fear
that our inner eyes
given to us for eternity
are less sure
than our outward sight
given us at birth
but tiring and fading with age?
Do we doubt this inner sight
because like new-born with their seeing
we have not much used it
and proved it to be true,
beyond even our understanding?
Let us know, O God,
with a certainty like the disciples' touch,
that it is you we see
at the heart of all things,
life everlasting,
and that our seeing may be more and more sure.
And when we doubt
let it be to doubt
that the outward eye

is the sole and final judge,
and wonder why we ever gave it such place,
for with inner eyes we see you, God,
not removed from life
but in it.

Silence

Let us pray for new ways of seeing
in our lives and relationships and world,
especially in places of fear:
for people in the midst of uncontrolled violence
and threatening disease;
for women and children and men
who are victims
of physical and emotional abuse;
and for all who face death
or who stand beside dying loved ones.
For ourselves
and for all people we pray, O God.
Increase our vision
that we may be more aware of you
even in the wounded side of life,
and that being more aware
we may in all things
more believe
and more hope.

THE SIXTH
Then he opened their minds to understand the scriptures.
Luke 24.45

Let us pray:

O God of our mothers and fathers
and of all who have gone before,

Author of the great book of life
whose secrets are written
in the unfolding universe
and in the smallest creatures of earth and sea,
and whose mysteries have been discerned in wisdom
by men and women through the centuries
and recorded in holy books
and etched in sacred places,
open our minds
that we may understand the Scriptures of life,
given that all may know your ways
and be guided in the journey of return to you.
We give thanks
that the story of salvation
which comes to us in Christ
is the truth implanted
in the whole of creation,
in the richness and history
of our traditions and peoples,
and in the depths of our own experiences,
the promise
of life out of death,
joy out of sorrow,
glory and new beginnings
out of chaos and failure.
Open our minds, O God,
to understand
that even out of sufferings
in our lives
and out of the apparent dead endings
in our world
you prepare a new path of life,
and to the repentant
provide a forgiveness
that will unlock a treasury of life
beyond our imagining.

Silence

Let us pray
for all who are in the midst
of difficult and bewildering times,
who have not been taught to read
the signs of God's hope
deep in life,
or have forgotten to look,
or are so enclosed
by the confusions of their difficulty
that they see only empty darkness or chaos:
for those who suffer an inward agony of mind or soul,
for those heartbroken by betrayal or loss,
for those who struggle against wrong
and lose hope of new beginnings.
We pray for your guidance for all people
and for all nations, O God,
asking that as we read and remember
the stories of your safeguarding and deliverance
in the past,
so may we know
with an inner assurance
your presence among us now,
and with a confidence
that is deeper than circumstance
believe in your providential care
and your provision now and forever.

THE SEVENTH
'I am sending upon you what my Father promised.'
Luke 24.49

Let us pray:

O God,
who called forth all life
from the seas and from the earth
and made us in your image,
breath of your breath,
life of your life,
we give thanks that in Christ
the promise has been spoken,
that like him
we too are your sons and daughters
conceived in heaven and born of earth,
that we too are beloved,
cherished by you and your holy angels,
and that we too in dying live
and are held in the company of the saints.
We give thanks
for the gift of the Holy Spirit
poured out continuously upon creation,
running through the flowing waters,
leaping in the living flames of the stars,
surging up green from the soil,
a rushing wind bearing life on its wings.
And we give thanks for the promise
that this poured-out Spirit
is the very Spirit that was in Christ,
gentle and forgiving,
mighty and righteous,
patient and true,
and that in and by that Spirit
we and every person on earth
may be clothed with the invincible power of love
which even death cannot overcome.

Silence

With the words of Christ's promise in us
we pray

for those who wait for its fulfilment in their lives,
who look for new births,
for beginnings out of endings,
for health out of illness,
peace out of conflict,
for life out of death.
We pray
for those who long for the freedom
and the creativity of the Spirit,
which comes from who knows where
and blows where it chooses:
for whole societies and nations bound by repression;
for men and women
whose intuition and flow of affection,
whose inner sight and creativity
are sealed off;
for children
whose natural openness to the Spirit
is discouraged or neglected;
and for those
who seek to comfort and heal in their societies,
to create justice and bring peace
as channels of the life-giving Spirit.
For all people,
for every family on earth
we pray,
asking for them
what we most desire for ourselves
and our loved ones,
the joy that comes from knowing that we are loved,
each one cherished as a child of promise.

APPENDIX:
OTHER SCRIPTURE CANTICLES

A SONG OF DAVID
Blessed are you, O Lord, God of our ancestors.
Yours is the glory, the victory, and the majesty.
For all that is in the heavens and on the earth is yours.
**Treasures and honour come from you, and you rule over
all things.**
It is in your hand to make great and to give strength.
**And now, our God, we give thanks to you and praise your
glory.**
(1 Chronicles 29)

VENITE
O come, let us sing to the Lord;
let us make a joyful noise to the rock of our salvation!
Let us come into his presence with thanksgiving;
let us make a joyful noise to him with songs of praise!
For the Lord is a great God,
and a great King above all gods.
In his hand are the depths of the earth;
the heights of the mountains are his also.
The sea is his, for he made it,
and the dry land, which his hands have formed.
O come, let us worship and bow down,
let us kneel before the Lord, our Maker!
For he is our God,
and we are the people of his pasture,
and the sheep of his hand.
O that today you would listen to his voice!
Do not harden your hearts as in the wilderness.
For he comes to judge the earth with righteousness,
and the peoples with his truth.
(Psalm 95)

JUBILATE
Make a joyful noise to the Lord, all the earth.
Worship the Lord with gladness;
come into his presence with singing.
Know that the Lord is God.
It is he that made us, and not we ourselves;
we are his people, and the sheep of his pasture.
Enter his gates with thanksgiving,
and his courts with praise.
Give thanks to him and bless his name.
For the Lord is good;
his steadfast love endures forever,
and his faithfulness to all generations.
(Psalm 100)

A SONG OF PEACE
Come, let us go up to the mountain of the Lord,
to the house of the God of Jacob;
that he may teach us his ways
and that we may walk in his paths.
He shall judge between the nations,
and shall arbitrate for the peoples.
They shall beat their swords into ploughshares,
and their spears into pruning hooks.
Nation shall not lift up sword against nation,
neither shall they learn war any more.
O house of Jacob,
let us walk in the light of the Lord.
(Isaiah 2)

A SONG OF RETURN
Seek the Lord while he may be found,
call upon him while he is near.
Let the wicked forsake their way,
and the unrighteous their thoughts.
Let them return to the Lord, that he may have mercy upon them,
to our God, for he will abundantly pardon.

For my thoughts are not your thoughts,
nor are your ways my ways, says the Lord.
For as the heavens are higher than the earth,
so are my ways higher than your ways
and my thoughts than your thoughts.
(Isaiah 55)

A SONG TO THE KING OF THE AGES
Blessed be God who lives forever,
and whose kingdom lasts throughout all ages.
He afflicts, and he shows mercy;
he leads down to the depths of the earth
and he lifts up from the great abyss.
Exalt him in the presence of every living being,
because he is our Lord and God forever.
He afflicted you for your iniquities,
but he will again show mercy.
If you turn to him with all your heart and soul,
then he will turn to you
and no longer hide his face from you.
Bless the Lord of righteousness,
and exalt the King of the ages.
(Tobit 13)

THE SONG OF ZECHARIAH (BENEDICTUS)
Blessed be the Lord God of Israel,
for he has looked favourably on his people and redeemed
them.
He has raised up a mighty saviour for us
in the house of his servant David,
as he spoke through the mouth of his holy prophets from of
old,
that we would be saved from our enemies and from the hand
of all who hate us.
Thus he has shown the mercy promised to our ancestors,
and has remembered his holy covenant,
the oath that he swore to our ancestor Abraham:
that we might be set free from the hands of our enemies,

to serve him without fear, in holiness and righteousness
all the days of our life.
And you, child, will be called the prophet of the Most High;
for you will go before the Lord to prepare his ways,
to give knowledge of salvation to his people
by the forgiveness of their sins.
By the tender mercy of our God,
the dawn from on high will break upon us,
to give light to those who sit in darkness and in the
shadow of death,
and to guide our feet into the way of peace.
(Luke 1)

A SONG OF CHRIST'S GLORY
Christ Jesus was in the form of God:
but he did not cling to equality with God.
He emptied himself, taking the form of a servant,
and was born in human likeness.
He humbled himself, and became obedient unto death,
even death on a cross.
Therefore God has highly exalted him:
and bestowed on him the name above all others,
that at the name of Jesus every knee should bow,
in heaven and on earth and under the earth;
and every tongue confess him Lord,
to the glory of God the Father.
(Philippians 2)

A SONG WITHOUT CEASING
Holy, holy, holy,
the Lord God Almighty,
who was and is and is to come.
You are worthy, Our Lord and God,
to receive glory and honour and power.
for you created all things
and by your will they exist.
(Revelation 4)